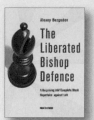

Contents

2015#1

NEW IN CHESS

'I like spicy and full of flavour. Please no bland Euro-food.'

CONTRIBUTORS TO THIS ISSUE
Vladimir Barsky, Jeroen Bosch, Adam Feinstein, Anish Giri, Alexander Grischuk, Robin van Kampen, Vladimir Kramnik, Igor Lysyj, Parimarjan Negi, Maxim Notkin, Alejandro Ramirez, Matthew Sadler, Nigel Short, Jonathan Speelman, Jan Timman, Maxime Vachier-Lagrave, Yu Yangyi

PHOTOS AND ILLUSTRATIONS
Alina l'Ami, Maria Emelianova, Eteri Kublashvili, David Llada, Ray Morris-Hill, Dmitry Rukhletsky, Gu Xiaobing

COVER
Miguel Najdorf, his daughters Mirta and Liliana, and Bobby Fischer

'Caruana doesn't seem to notice his opponent at all. Perhaps that's why he's one of the toughest rivals for Carlsen - because he seems impervious to the psychology that haunts most of us.' – *Parimarjan Negi*

NIC's Café

Alexander's Enigma

As Tinseltown readies itself to once again roll out the big red carpet on February 22nd, here at the Café, we're tipping Benedict Cumberbatch as a serious candidate for an Oscar for his portrayal in *The Imitation Game* of mathematics genius Alan Turing. The biopic reveals how, during World War II, while stationed at the highly secretive Bletchley Park, Turing set his mind to cracking the German Naval cipher Enigma, which ultimately played an invaluable role in the Battle of the Atlantic.

Turing's task in breaking the code was made easier by the assistance of some of Britain's top chess players of the time, the most notable one being Hugh Alexander, his deputy at Bletchley's legendary Hut 8, who later went on to become head of crypto-analysis at the top British government intelligence station GCHQ. In the movie, Alexander – a man of Anglo-Irish descent whose full name was Conel Hugh O'Donel Alexander (known at

Alan Turing (Benedict Cumberbatch) surrounded by colleagues in Hut 8. On the right C.H.O'D. Alexander (Matthew Goode).

Bletchley as C.H.O'D) – is one of the main characters, played by Cumberbatch's co-star Matthew Goode.

We will refrain from spoiler alerts, but what we will say is that the movie is well worth viewing, not only for its backstory, but also for the working

Today we know why C.H.O'D Alexander never became Britain's first grandmaster.

relationship that developed between Turing and Alexander, who becomes something of a cultured counterpoint to the film's doomed hero.

Alexander was a two-time British champion, and many believe he had the talent to become Britain's first grandmaster, decades before Tony Miles did so in 1976. But breaking this enigma as to why he didn't is an easy one: the extremely high-security clearance of his postwar work denied him the chance to do so. As one of his country's leading Cold War players, the British government never allowed Alexander to play in a Soviet bloc country for fear of being kidnapped or compromised by the KGB.

A pity, really, because Alexander had the mind-set and skills required to beat many of the world's leading players. His most famous victories were against Soviet titans Mikhail Botvinnik, during the 1946 Anglo-Soviet Radio Match, and David Bronstein, at Hastings in 1953/54 – a marathon encounter that lasted for days and was followed eagerly in the front pages of the British press. Alexander then went on to crush former Soviet champion Alexander Tolush in the final round to share first place with Bronstein, then the world's number two.

When Alexander died in 1974 at the age of 64 – and many say the reasons for his early death were stress and pressure from his work – Botvinnik described him as 'a great chess player – he will never be forgotten.'

Spring is Coming...

Last year, when Magnus Carlsen won the Rapid and Blitz world titles in Dubai, thus becoming the first player to hold the triple crown in chess, cartoonist José Diaz worked his magic around a theme on the popular HBO fantasy drama, *Game of Thrones*.

And from 23 to 29 January, GoT is set to get the silver screen treatment by becoming the first TV series to be shown in IMAX cinemas. But it will not so much be a case of winter but rather spring that's coming, with two specially remastered episodes in the IMAX format from season four set to precede the first trailer for the much-anticipated arrival of season five, due in early April.

What's all this got to do with chess, you might ask? Quite a lot, as rabid

Magnus 'Game of Thrones' Carlsen by José Diaz.

GoT fans who frequent the Café have discovered. In a major interview in the UK last year for *The Independent Magazine* with George R.R. Martin, the GoT creator revealed that we have to thank chess for his emergence as a writer, which led directly to the cult series. At his peak as a player, Martin was one rank below that of 'master' in the US chess-rating system. The importance of chess to Martin, though, was not as a player but as a tournament director.

In the early 1970s, his big dream was to be a full-time writer – but he needed a job to support himself until his fiction could. Then Bobby Fischer beat Boris Spassky, which created a chess boom in America. Martin was hired full-time to direct the Midwestern tournament circuit. 'For two or three years, I had a pretty good situation,' explains Martin. 'Most writers who have to have a day job work

Without chess George R.R. Martin might never have created the incredibly popular *Game of Thrones*.

five days a week and then they have the weekend off to write. These chess tournaments were all on the weekends… I had five days off to write.'

After a year or two, the American chess bubble burst. There was no longer much money in setting up tournaments. 'But, by then, I was much better established as a writer,' he reflects. 'The chess really did mark a crucial turning point in my career.'

Life of a King

What with *The Imitation Game*, *Game of Thrones* and now the television premier this month of the chess-centric melodrama *Life of a King*, you could be forgiven for thinking that the only thing we read in our editorial meetings these days is *Variety* – but the popular entertainment-trade magazine continues to be an invaluable source of chess material these days, as our game continues to be popular in the pop culture scene.

The uplifting movie is inspired by the powerful and true story of Eugene

Brown (played by Cuba Gooding Jr.), a Washington D.C. ex-con who was incarcerated for 18 years in a federal prison for a botched bank robbery. Chess, which Eugene picked up from his prison mentor, offers Eugene convenient life lessons about rules, perseverance and mindfulness. On his release, he went on to become the inspirational founder of the Big Chair Chess Club Inc. (bigchairchessclub.com). His mission was to reach out to inner-city at-risk kids to get them off the streets in the 1990s, kids who had been largely written off by society, and in whom he instils his motto 'Always Think Before You Move' through chess as a way to avoid the 'Big House' later in life.

Academy Award winner Gooding Jr. is especially good as the central character in this very watchable movie with a moral tale. He plays a character that is not just struggling to go straight and to reconnect with his estranged children – one of whom is also in jail – but also to find his grand purpose in life – and he does, through chess.

Brown has a cameo appearance in the movie, wearing his trade-

Life of a King, an uplifting movie inspired by a powerful and true story.

mark black and white chequered cap. 'When I teach chess, I always get the kids to identify themselves as the king,' explains Brown. 'One thing about being the king: You are the

Eugene Brown has a cameo appearance wearing his trademark black and white chequered cap.

thinker – male or female… Because when the game was first explained to me, and I really had to accept all of the blame, and I couldn't really blame anybody else. I had kind of run out of excuses. And when I accepted my kingship for all the moves I made, then my life changed dramatically. *Life of a King* is the life of a thinker.'

Sorry, Nigel

For reasons beyond our comprehension the final standings of the Isle of Man tournament that we published in our previous issue (p. 64) were seriously flawed. The winner was indeed Nigel Short, but he didn't finish a teeny-weeny half point ahead of a group of seven players. Of course not. He did much better! In actual fact, our esteemed columnist (7½/9) collected a full point more than Fressinet, Tiviakov, Howell and Popilski. And Adams, Vachier-Lagrave and Sargissian were amongst the players that finished in 6th-11th place with six points. All we can do is apologize. Sorry, Nigel. ■

Yu Yangyi topples favourites in inaugural Qatar Masters Open

A daily ritual in the early rounds. Vladimir Kramnik checks the name of his opponent and makes sure he spells it correctly.

How about this scenario? Top-seed Anish Giri bursts away with six straight wins until he is stopped by former World Champion Vladimir Kramnik, who is playing his first Open in 21 years. The Russian also wins six games on the trot and takes over the lead. Game over? Not really. Enter former Junior World Champion Yu Yangyi. The Chinese GM beats both Giri and Kramnik in his last two games to claim another victory in his young and burgeoning career. A bit far-fetched? Perhaps. Still, this is exactly what happened at the Qatar Masters Open in Doha. Dutch GM **Robin van Kampen** watched it all and tells the tale.

Piece of cake. Kramnik and Giri secure their dessert with a traditional sword. Yu Yangyi seems to be counting calories and patiently waits for the trophy and the winner's check.

When I signed up in July for the newly announced Qatar Open, I cherished some ambitions of winning the tournament. With a rating of 2600 and some change I was expecting to be ranked around the top-10. Just some flashy tournament in the Middle East with good prizes and a relatively weak field, right? It was only when the Olympiad came around and Anish Giri mentioned to me that he would be meeting GM Al-Modiahki that suspicions began racing through my head. Word soon began to spread, and it became clear that the organizers in Qatar were pulling out all the stops and were all set to organize a top Open. Resigned to my fate, I slowly watched my name getting pushed down the starting list week by week. It was as if a large chess Colosseum was being constructed in Doha with the main intention of having dozens and dozens of grandmasters battle each other to death. Whether it was the attractive prizes, or tourism, or glory, in the end

over a hundred grandmasters made the trek to Doha to duel it out.

Besides the vast majority of 'dreamers' (read: players rated around 2650 or less) hoping to win the tournament, there were a few hard-to-miss juggernauts like Kramnik, Mamedyarov, Vachier-Lagrave, and Giri. While most 2700+ players are occasional participants in open tournaments, Big Vlad had taken an extended holiday from them. In fact, the last time Kramnik was seen in an Open was in 1993, when kids like Anish and yours truly were yet to roam the Earth. Enough reason for more than a few people to think that the former World Champion would be rusty.

Winning an Open like the Qatar Masters is a whole different ball game compared to the closed events that many top players are accustomed to. Instead of conceding draws as Black it's often necessary to take risks and play for a win to keep up with the leaders. One thing was for certain:

there would be a lot of upsets and exciting games!

Let me guide you through the first Qatar Masters, which ended in an extraordinary and thrilling finale. My main emphasis will be on the journeys of the top three finishers.

Halkias-Kramnik
Doha 2014 (1)
position after 17..♕c6

18.♕g4

Facing the unusual Evans Gambit, Kramnik managed to get a decent position, but after his next move things went downhill for him.

18...♖ad8?!
After 18...♕c4 19.♕h3 ♖fe8 20.♗g5 h5!, with the idea of ...♗g4, Black would have been slightly better.

19.♗g5 Now White has a small initiative and easy piece play.

19...♕c5 20.♕h4 ♞c6 21.♖ae1 h5 22.♖e4
Possibly more dangerous was 22.♕f4, with ideas of ♗f6.

22...♖d3 Better was 22...♗xg5! 23.♕xg5 ♖fe8, and Black is in time to play 24...♕f8 in reply to 24.♕h6.

23.♖c4 ♕d5 24.♗xe7 ♞xe7 25.♖xc7
Black has some activity, but this can hardly be called compensation for the pawn.

25...♞f5

26.♕c4?!
26.♕f4 would have posed Black more problems, as there will always be ideas of attacking the black knight.

26...♕xc4 27.♖xc4 ♖e8 28.♖e1
White is still a pawn up, but it is difficult to convert it to something tangible, and the game soon ended in a draw.

A bit of a disappointing start for Kramnik, but the Greek grandmaster played a good game. In his second game the Russian Super GM came closer, but again his significantly lower-rated opponent played well.

RE 12.3 – A13
Vladimir Kramnik
Sundar Shyam
Doha 2014 (2)

1.♞f3 d5 2.c4 e6 3.b3 ♗e7 4.♗b2 ♗f6 5.♞c3 dxc4 6.bxc4 c5 7.g4 h6 8.h4

No need to play it solid!
8...♗d7 9.e3 ♗c6 10.♗g2 ♞d7

11.♔e2!? Connecting the major pieces, preparing g5 and a good prophylactic move against Black's idea of ...♗xf3, ...♞e5, ...♞d3+.

11...♔f8 Another showy king move. Black's idea is to take on c3 and play ...e5, which should create some *luft* for his pieces, whilst strengthening his control of the centre. Yet, developing the bishop to f6 only to exchange it off on c3 a few moves later seems dubious, and perhaps 11...♞e7 12.g5 ♗e5 was to be preferred.

12.g5 ♗xc3 13.♗xc3 e5 14.d4 exd4 15.exd4 ♗xf3+ 16.♗xf3

White should stand clearly better due to his bishops and slight lead in development. Do those principles still count with oddly-placed kings? I guess they do!
16...hxg5 17.♗xb7 ♕e7+ 18.♔f1 ♖d8

19.hxg5
Here 19.♕d2!, preparing to deploy the last major piece on e1, would have landed Black in serious trouble, e.g. 19...♖xh4 (after 19...gxh4 20.♖e1 ♕d6 21.dxc5 ♞xc5 22.♕xd6+ ♖xd6 23.♗f3 Black is in big trouble, as ♗b4 is coming) 20.♖e1 ♞e5 21.♖xh4 gxh4 22.♖h1 f6 23.♕b2, with complications favouring White.

19...♖xh1+ 20.♗xh1 ♕xg5

Now Black is only slightly worse. Fast forward! Kramnik gets another good opportunity to win the game.

21.♕f3 ♘gf6 22.♖e1 ♕h4 23.♗g2 cxd4 24.♗b4+ ♔g8 25.♗e7 ♖e8 26.♕f5 ♕h7 27.♕xh7+ ♔xh7 28.c5 d3 29.♗d6 d2 30.♖d1 ♘e4 31.c6 ♘b6

32.♗f4?!

Instead, 32.♗b4! would have got Black into real trouble, the main point being: 32...f5 (after 32...♘c4 33.c7 is now possible, as Black has no 33...♘c3) 33.♗xd2 ♖c8 34.♗xe4 fxe4 35.♖c1 is clearly better for White.

32...♘c4 33.♗xe4+ ♖xe4 34.c7 ♖e8 35.♗xd2 ♘xd2+ 36.♖xd2 ♖c8

And a draw was agreed a few moves later.

After his lacklustre 50 per cent start, things began to get a bit worrying for Kramnik. If he couldn't beat guys whom he had never heard of, then how was he supposed to compete? Things only started falling into place for the Russian Super GM when, after a long struggle in Round 3, he managed to bring home the bacon in his pet Berlin.

In the meantime, I had managed to win my first game and was getting paired up in the second round. Along with my fellow 2600 'amateurs' I was going to have to face the 2700 bullies. What cannot be cured must be endured and luckily a few upsets are bound to happen in such situations. This time, I found myself on the right side of a surprising result ☺.

Das Debashis, always happy to help, shows Vladimir Kramnik his name. The Russian won and would win his next five games as well.

'If he couldn't beat guys whom he had never heard of, then how was Kramnik supposed to compete?'

RL 26.10 – C92
**Robin van Kampen
Ding Liren**
Doha 2014 (2)

1.e4 e5 2.♘f3 ♘c6 3.♗b5 a6 4.♗a4 ♘f6 5.0-0 ♗e7 6.♖e1 b5 7.♗b3 d6 8.c3 0-0 9.h3 ♖e8 10.d4 ♗b7 11.♘bd2 ♗f8

12.d5

I generally play 12.a3 here, but fearing my opponent's preparation, I decided to play an old line, hoping we would both be on our own sooner or later.

12...♘b8 13.♘f1 ♘bd7 14.♘3h2

Standard manoeuvring in these types of positions. The entire position revolves around Black playing ...c6 and White trying to control the d5-square.

14...c6!? The only line known to me was 14...♘c5 15.♗c2 c6, after which Black is generally experiencing no real problems either.

15.dxc6 ♗xc6 16.♗g5 ♕c7 17.♕f3

Played quickly. At first I thought my position looked quite good. If White gets time to exchange on f6 and play ♘g4, followed by ♘e3-d5, he will dominate. But my opponent was well prepared.

17...a5!

Our reporter Robin van Kampen found himself on the right side of a surprising result in his game against Chinese ace Ding Liren.

18.♗xf6

The move White would like to make is 18.a3, but after 18...♘c5! the bishop and e4 are hanging: 19.♗c2 ♘fd7, followed by ...♘e6, hitting the bishop on g5. Black is doing well.

18...♘xf6 19.♘g4 ♘xg4 20.hxg4 a4 21.♗c2

The position that has arisen is nothing to write home about. As you can see, White is quite far from controlling the d5-square with two pieces, and Black can comfortably develop his f8-bishop to the g5-square. Here my opponent started thinking for the first time, and after a while came up with the surprising:

21...♖e6

This move is among the computer's top choices, but it really makes little sense to me compared to 21...♗e7 22.♘e3 ♗g5 23.♖ad1 ♗xe3, when Black has comfortably equalized. Or 23...♗d7 24.♘d5 ♕a7, with an unclear position. My guess is that my opponent recalled this move from his analysis, but soon after this he started to drift, and with every move his position got worse and worse.

22.♖ad1 a3 23.b4 ♗d7

24.♖d3 Preparing ♕d1, both defending g4 and preparing ♗b3.
24...♖f6 25.♕d1 ♗e6 26.♗b3 ♕a7 27.♘e3 Now White is clearly better. At any moment ♘d5 is possible, when the opposite-coloured bishop positions are clearly unpleasant, since f7 and b5 are future targets. In the meantime, it still isn't clear what Black has achieved by putting his rook on f6.

27...g6

28.♕e2

Much stronger was 28.g5! ♖f4 (28...♗xb3 29.♕xb3 ♖e6 30.c4! is also close to winning. Or at least, it looks like a text-book example of Bad Bishop versus Good Knight ☺) 29.♗d5 ♗xd5 30.♖xd5 ♖xe4 31.g3!, followed by ♕d3, was much stronger, picking up the exchange, as the stray e4-rook is short of squares.

28...♗xb3?! 29.axb3 a2 30.♖a1

Now it's just a matter of picking up the a2- or b5-pawn.

30...♗h6 31.♘d5 ♖e6 32.♖dd1 ♗g5 33.♕xb5

And Black resigned a few moves later. There is no way to use the a2-pawn, and White can easily move away his queen and advance with b5-b6, when the win is trivial.

Sometimes you just meet the right opponent at the right time! Up to this point, the biggest challenge had been reaching the playing hall both safely and on time. The Qatari people seem to be fond of fancy cars, which led to dangerous situations when absent-minded chess players were crossing the busy roads to reach the playing hall.

Following my auspicious start, I soon found myself back among the proletariat playing catch-up. Whilst many top players struggled in the first few rounds, my two good friends GM Nils Grandelius from Sweden and GM Anish Giri from the Netherlands grabbed the lead with impressive winning streaks.

When in good form, Anish has the tendency to walk around a lot, occasionally come over to my board, dissect my position for a while and raise his eyebrows. By way of compensation I sometimes try to do the same thing, but in Qatar I had little to raise my eyebrows about.

The following game of Anish stood out for me – a crushing 21-move win with black over Azerbaijan's Shakhriyar Mamedyarov in Round 4.

EO 11.5 – A22
Shakhriyar Mamedyarov
Anish Giri
Doha 2014 (5)

1.c4 ♘f6 2.♘c3 e5 3.g3 ♗b4 4.♗g2 0-0 5.e4

A reversed Rossolimo Sicilian has arisen.

5...♗xc3 6.bxc3 I'm not a huge fan of this recapture. The main reason is that Black gets easy play in the centre.

> 'When in good form, Anish has the tendency to walk around a lot, occasionally come over to my board, dissect my position for a while and raise his eyebrows.'

6.dxc3 leads to a totally different game with a more closed character.
6...♖e8 7.d3 c6!

The main reason why not too many people play this line with White. Black plans to open up the centre with ...d5, when his lead in development has been proven to compensate for the relinquished bishop.
8.♘e2
8.♗g5 was tried by Andreikin in 2012, but after the simple 8...h6 9.♗xf6 ♕xf6 10.♘e2 d6 the position was roughly equal.
8...d5 9.cxd5 cxd5 10.exd5 ♘xd5

11.♖b1 A novelty. More common is 11.0-0, but after 11...♗g4! 12.♗d2, 12...♘c6, followed by ...♕d7 and ...♗h3, is very comfortable for Black.
11...♘c6 12.0-0
12.♕c2 deserved attention, as 12...♗g4 can now be met by 13.♖xb7.
12...♗g4 13.f3

The critical position. If Black is forced to return to c8, White is doing alright, as he will eventually free his light-squared bishop by playing f3-f4. However, Anish had something sharper in mind, and managed to seize the initiative.
13...♗f5! 14.♖xb7 ♘b6 15.f4
Forced, as the rook is close to being lost on b7.
15...e4

16.♕b3? But this loses material. Correct was the cool 16.dxe4! ♗xe4 17.♕b3 ♕f6, when it seems as though ...♘a5 will win material; but White is in time after 18.♗xe4 ♖xe4 19.♘d4 ♘a5 20.♕c2! ♖xd4 (or 20...♖ee8 21.♖c7 ♕d6 22.♘b5 ♕d5 23.♘xa7!?, and the rook is still far from trapped!) 21.♖xb6 (the rook gets out just on time) 21...axb6 22.cxd4 ♕xd4+ 23.♕f2, with equality.

16...♗e6 White has no good defence against both ...exd3 and ...♗c8.
17.♕b5
17.♕d1 ♗c8 loses the exchange.
17...exd3 18.♖xb6 dxe2 19.♖e1

19...♗c4! A clever intermezzo, forcing White to take on c6 with the queen.
20.♕xc6 ♕d1 21.♔f2 ♖ad8
And seeing ...♕xe1+, followed by ...♖d1+, Shakh decided to call it a day.

The two young leaders eventually crossed swords in Round 6. For a long time the game seemed to be heading for a draw, but Anish showed strong willpower. He kept finding the most unpleasant moves until Nils finally cracked and lost. When I saw Nils after the prolonged torture he was in good spirits and quipped 'This Anish guy, he is quite good!'

Giri-Grandelius
Doha 2014 (6)
position after 51..♔f7

52.♔e3 ♘f6 There is nothing wrong with this move, but Nils could have released the tension with 52...♘d6! 53.♖xa6 (53.♖c5 ♖xc5 54.♘xc5 ♘c4+ 55.♔e4 e6! also equalizes) 53...♘c4+ 54.♔e4 ♖b5!, keeping the rooks on and not allowing the king to come to f5. On the next move Black can recapture the pawn on a5, after which the draw is close.
53.♖xa6 ♘xg4+ 54.♔e4 ♖d8 55.f3 ♘f6+ 56.♔e3

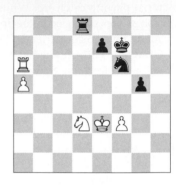

Black is still far from lost, but defending without having a clear plan how to eliminate the a-pawn is unpleasant.

56...♘d5+ 57.♔f2 e6 58.♖c6 ♖b8 59.♘e5+ ♔e7 60.♖c2 ♖b5?! 60...♖a8 61.♖a2 ♖a6 should have been enough for a draw.
61.a6

61...♘b4? Finally, Nils collapses under the pressure. Instead, 61...♘b6! 62.♘c6+ ♔d6 63.a7 ♘a8, with the idea of ...♖c5, would still be holding.
62.a7 ♖a5 63.♖b2
And Black can't move his knight due to the ♘c6+ fork.
63...♔f6 64.♘g4+ ♔f5 65.♘e3+ ♔f6 66.♖xb4 And White soon won.

Who was going to stop Giri? There are very few players left with a good record against Anish, and at this point he was a full point ahead of the field. Fortunately for the spectators, Kramnik had got into his stride and was mowing down GM's left and right on his way back to the top boards. Take a look at how he dismantled Russian talent Sanan Sjugirov.

RE 26.13 – A05
Vladimir Kramnik
Sanan Sjugirov
Doha 2014 (6)

1.♘f3 ♘f6 2.g3
Kramnik sticks to his 'no theoretical battle' approach. Or at least, that's what he tries to make us believe!
2...d5 3.♗g2 c6
The normal way for Slav-players to handle the KID Attack.
4.d3 ♗g4 5.0-0 ♘bd7 6.♕e1 e5 7.e4
A line that Kramnik had previously used to beat Vitiugov in 2013.

7...♗d6!? A rare move. Here 7...dxe4 is almost exclusively played, and the reason why is probably the game's continuation.
8.h3 ♗h5
8...♗xf3 9.♗xf3 is solid, but giving the bishop up so easily is admitting to a slight opening failure.
9.♘h4 0-0
It's too late for 9...dxe4 because of 10.♘f5!, hitting both g7 and d6.

10.g4! A pawn is a pawn!
10...♗g6 11.g5 ♘h5 12.exd5 cxd5 13.♘xg6 hxg6 14.♗xd5

White is a clear pawn up, but in return his king is somewhat exposed and he's behind in development.
14...♘f4 15.♗xf4 exf4 16.h4 ♕c8

Attacking c2 and at the same time eyeing the g4-square.
17.♕e4!
A strong centralizing move, giving back the pawn; but now it is Black's king that is going to be weakened.

17...♕xc2
17...♖e8!? was an interesting alternative, when 18.♗xb7 (after 18.♕xg6 ♘e5! 19.♕e4

ANALYSIS DIAGRAM

19...♘g6!! is an amazing resource, placing a second piece en prise on g6, but reaching a draw after 20.♕xg6 ♕g4+ 21.♔h1 ♕xh4+ 22.♔g1 ♕g4+) 18...♕c7 19.♗c6 leaves White with two pawns up. However, after 19...♖ac8! 20.♕xc7 ♖xc7 21.♗d5 ♖xc2 Black is still a pawn down, though it shouldn't make much difference thanks to his active pieces.
18.♘c3!?
18.♘a3 was a safer option. After 18...♗xa3 19.bxa3 ♕c5 20.d4 ♕xa3 21.♗xb7 ♖ad8 22.♕xf4 ♘b6 Black can create sufficient counterplay, e.g. 23.♗g2 ♘d5 24.♕d2 f6!.
18...♕xb2 19.♕xg6

19...♗c5

A safer way for Black was 19...♕xc3! 20.♕xd6 ♖ad8 21.♖ac1 ♕a5 22.♗e4 b6, intending ...♘c5xe4, with approximate equality.

19...♗e5?! is no good for Black either: 20.♕h5! ♕xc3 21.g6 ♖fc8 22.♗xf7+ ♔f8 23.♖ae1, with a winning attack.

20.♘e4

Hitting the bishop on c5 with tempo. White's main idea is ♕f5 and g6, with mating ideas.

20...♕e5?!

This is only helping White. Now, after putting a rook on e1, ♘f6+!, winning the queen, will be the threat.

20...♗e7 21.♕f5 ♕e5! 22.♕xd7 ♖ad8 (winning back the piece) 23.♗xf7+ ♖xf7 24.♕h3 ♗f8 is unpleasant for Black, but it's far from over.

21.♗b3 ♗xf2+

Desperation, but it was difficult to give Black any advice. 21...♗e7 brings no relief either: 22.♖ae1 ♕b5 23.♘d6 ♗xd6 24.♕xd6 ♖ad8 25.g6, and Black is helpless against the threats on the light squares.

22.♘xf2 f3 23.♘e4 ♕d4+ 24.♔h1 ♕b2

25.♘f6+! Black resigned. A nice end to the game. After 25...♘xf6 26.gxf6 the queen on g6 threatens mate on g7, while at the same time preventing it on g2.

And so the big day came when the two titans clashed. In Round 7, blood was surely going to be spilled. Big Vlad had regained his appetite with five straight wins and was eager to face his favourite afternoon snack, Mr. Giri. Here's that game with notes by the legend himself!

NOTES BY
Vladimir Kramnik

SL 6.2 – D43
Vladimir Kramnik
Anish Giri
Doha 2014 (7)

This game was played at an interesting moment; in the seventh round. Anish had 6 out of 6 and I was one point behind on 5 out of 6. We had won our last 10 games, he six in a row, and I four. If Anish didn't lose, he would probably go on to claim victory.

1.d4 So far I had played three Réti's, so I guess Anish had prepared for this seriously. That's why I decided to surprise him with this somewhat old-fashioned move, which I still play from time to time.

1...d5 2.c4 c6 3.♘f3 ♘f6 4.♘c3 e6

5.g3

In Open tournaments you don't have too much time to prepare. Nor do you prepare before the tournament, as you do before a round-robin. And since my opponent plays almost all the openings on the planet (against me he had already played the King's Indian, the Grünfeld, the Slav with ...dxc4, and other things), the only thing I could do was to think briefly what I might do against any opening he might choose. Just before the game, I decided to go for 5.g3, as I realized that he had never faced this before in his life. But I didn't have the time to really repeat everything, which may explain why I mixed up the move-order a bit further on.

5...dxc4 6.♗g2 b5 7.♘e5

7...a6

This was supposed to be the most reliable weapon against 5.g3, since 8.♘xc6 won't yield anything now because of 8...♕b6, and Black has no problem at all.

8.0-0 ♗b7 9.b3

This is what computers have started playing recently, a strange-looking pawn sacrifice which is actually pretty dangerous. Even though Black is doing fine in the end, I think it gives White quite a serious initiative.

9...cxb3

A very principled move is 9...b4, and I had quite some analysis there, but I don't think Anish knew about the 9.b3 idea, and in that case 9...b4 is not a move you make easily, knowing that your opponent is well prepared.

10.axb3 ♗e7 11.♗b2

It looks as if Black is a healthy pawn up, and if he manages to complete his development, he'll just be better. But when you start analysing this position, you quickly find that it's quite difficult for him to finish his development. And of course, if he plays half the game with his knight on b8 and his rook on a8, White will definitely have good compensation, even more so because it is also difficult for Black to push ...c5. This is the justification of the pawn sacrifice.

11...0-0 12.♕c2

Played rather quickly and just a Fingerfehler. In my analysis I wanted to play 12.♘e4 because now there is no 12...♘bd7 in view of 13.♘xc6.

Anish Giri shows Vladimir Kramnik who he is playing in Round 7. Inspired by his opponent's name the Russian won a brilliant game.

12...♘fd7

Immediately after I had played the queen to c2, I realized that Black has the strong 12...♘bd7!, when there is no way for White to play for an advantage and he just has to equalize with 13.♗xc6 (13.♘xc6 ♗xc6 14.♗xc6 ♖c8, and the bishop goes back and ...b4 is coming, while after 15.♖xa6 there is 15...♘b8) 13...♕c8 14.♗xb7 ♕xb7, and Black is slightly better, but the position is very drawish.

Anish didn't notice my mistake, and now the game continues as it normally should have. He spent quite some time on this move, giving me a tough time, as I was cursing myself for mixing up the move order. I was walking around in a cold sweat telling myself what an idiot I was to spoil this chance on move 12. I was quite

far away from the board, and when I turned back, I saw that he had moved and that there was a knight on d7, which made me feel quite down. But when I got closer, I suddenly saw that he had moved the other knight to d7, which was such a relief.

13.♘d3

It's also possible to start with 13.♘e4, as I don't think Black can play 13...♘xe5, since after 14.dxe5 I get a strong initiative with my knight coming to d6, but I thought that after 13...a5 14.♖fc1 ♕b6 15.♘d3 the game would develop more or less the same as in the game.

13...♕b6 14.♘e4

I have stopped ...c5, and the knight on b8 is not feeling very comfortable.

14...a5 A very logical move, trying to develop pieces.

Following the success of the first Qatar Masters Open, there are plans for a second edition at the end of this year.

MARIA EMELIANOVA

15.♘dc5

A somewhat unnatural move, played after about 45 minutes – and quite a surprise to my opponent as far as I could judge from his mimics. As the knight on d3 looks good, the most logical move seems to be 15.♘ec5, but the problem was that after 15...♘xc5 I could not see a clear way to proceed. My compensation is good enough for equality, but no more: 16.♘xc5 (after 16.dxc5 ♕c7 17.♗e5 ♕d8 18.♖fd1 ♘d7 I don't see why White should be really better here) 16...♗c8 (Black's position looks ugly, but he is also a pawn up, There is no immediate threat for White, however)

ANALYSIS DIAGRAM

17.♖fc1 (another way to try and create pressure was 17.♕e4, but then Black just slowly manoeuvres his pieces: 17...♖a7 18.♖fc1 ♖d8 19.♗c2 (19.e3 ♖c7) 19...♖c7, preparing ...♘d7, and I will probably get my pawn back at some point, with a draw) 17...♘a6 (giving back the pawn and steering for a position that looks pretty drawish) 18.♘xa6 ♖xa6 19.♕xc6 ♕b8 20.♕c7 ♕xc7 21.♖xc7 ♗d6 22.♖c6 b4, and this is just a draw.

15...♗c8

After this move I would prefer my knight to be on d3, but you can't get everything in life. After 15...♘xc5 I play 16.dxc5, and after 16...♕c7 17.♕c3 f6 18.♖fd1 ♘a6 19.♗h3 ♗c8 20.♘d6 Black is in quite serious trouble here.

An interesting option was 15...f5, which is quite a committal move but not that bad: 16.♘xe6 fxe4 17.♘xf8 ♘xf8 18.♕xe4 ♗f6 19.♖fc1 ♗c8, and to my taste White should be better in the long run. Once my central pawns start running, this should be quite painful for Black.

16.♕c3

I spent quite some time here – another 30 minutes. White has to be very accurate to keep his initiative going. Another possibility was 16.♖fc1, but after 16...♘a6 17.♕d2 (17.♕c3 b4 18.♕e3 leads to the game) 17...♘c7

18.♘xd7 ♗xd7 19.♘c5 ♗e8 20.♗c3 b4 21.♗b2 ♘b5 there is not much difference with the game.

16...b4 17.♕e3 ♘a6 18.♖fc1

Maybe I could have played 18.♖fd1, but then I decided it would not make much sense, since he would play 18...♘c7 (of course he is not going to take on c5), and the rook is not so great on d1.

18...♘c7

Strangely enough, the computer says that things are not so bad after 18...♘axc5 19.dxc5 ♕c7 20.♘d6 ♗a6. During the game I thought I had a very powerful initiative. But it's not so easy to break through. Let's say 21.♗d4 ♖fd8, and Black may not have too many ideas in this position, but it's not easy to improve for White. Maybe I can just start pushing my pawns with h4. This leaves Black passive, since he can never take on d6. But 18...♘c7 is much more human.

19.♘xd7 ♗xd7 20.♘c5

20...♗e8

The bishop is forced back. This is an important point. If the rook on f8 would be on, say, d8, Black would not be worse at all, but his problem is that his rook is closed in. White has no threats, nor a real plan to improve his position, but it's very difficult to make moves for Black. This is an important aspect of chess. Very often it is not about who is objectively better, but whose play is more difficult.

21.♖a2 ♕b5

Basically, Black doesn't have any real plan here; he has to more or less just stay put, waiting for White to do something and then reacting.

22.♕d3

Objectively, 22.♕e4 may have been better, followed by e3, h4, just slow, slow play, but since I only had about two minutes left here, I took a practical decision by offering the queen swap. It seems that it was the right decision. I am not sure I would have taken it 10 or 15 years ago. Facing a young and energetic player, the only real trump I have is experience.

22...♕xd3

There was the ugly option of 22...♗xc5, which neither of us considered very seriously, because giving up such a bishop looks strange; but it seems as if this allows Black to hold, so maybe it was better than the text-move: 23.♕xb5 ♘xb5 24.♖xc5 ♖a6 25.e4 (although the computer indicates that the position is equal, I am brave enough to disagree) 25...f6 26.♗f1 (White has full control and slowly starts playing for compensation) 26...♗f7 27.f3 ♖fa8 28.♔f2 ♔f8 29.♗c4, followed by ♔e3 and maybe g4 and h4, and it's obvious that from a human point of view the position is very nice for White and no one would deliberately play it with Black.

23.♘xd3 ♘d5 24.♘e5

I actually thought I was already better here, since Black's position is becoming dangerous.

24...♖a6

According to Anish, he had just missed my reply. The computer thinks that after 24...c5 25.dxc5 ♗b5 Black will more or less hold. I saw this resource, but it looks bad for Black, as I am getting a passed c-pawn and get my pawn back, but it's not easy to prove: 26.e4 (after the slow 26.♗d4 ♖fc8 27.♘d3 Black should also hold) 26...♘c3 27.♗xc3 bxc3 28.♖xc3 ♖fc8 29.c6. This is a far better version than what finally happened in the game, but it's not yet a complete draw. Still, after 29...♗b4 30.♖c1 f6 31.♘c4 Black is closer to a draw than White is to a win.

25.♗f1

A very powerful move. Now Black is in real trouble. All of a sudden his

position starts collapsing. He thought for a long time and basically panicked.

25...♘c3 On the other hand, it's not easy to offer anything better. Maybe 25...♘c7 could be played. But the following variation, which is very logical and almost forced, shows how difficult Black's position is: 26.e3 ♘b5 27.♘c4 ♗d8 28.♖ca1 (I'm already getting my pawn back) 28...♖a7 29.♘xa5 ♘c3 30.♗xc3 bxc3 31.♘c4 ♖xa2 32.♖xa2 (and I am picking up the c3-pawn) 32...♗e7 33.♖c2 ♗b4 34.♘e5, followed by ♘d3, and we will end up four pawns against four pawns with an extra b-pawn for me. There's still some technical work to be done, but it's clear that Black's position is difficult.

26.♗xc3 bxc3 27.♖xc3

A dream Catalan position. Just look at all Black's weaknesses.

27...c5

An attempt to get out with his pieces, but it's a little too late already.

But what else? After 27...♗b4 28.♖c1 f6 29.e3 ♖b6 30.♘d3 it seems to me that sooner or later we will end up in a five vs. four endgame with rook and bishop vs. rook and bishop; a very difficult, if not losing, endgame for Black.

28.dxc5 ♗f6 29.f4 ♗b5

30.♗g2

A powerful move. Here I hesitated. The simplest move was 30.e3, and I almost made it, but then I thought that Black might get some chances after 30...♗xf1 31.♔xf1 ♗xe5 32.fxe5 ♖c8 33.♖c4 ♖aa8. I think this should be slowly but surely winning for White. I can take my king to a4, and there is the manoeuvre ♖d2-d4, but it's a rook endgame, and rook endgames are always drawn, as I was told as a child – although I have my doubts about this one.

30...♖a7 31.c6

It was also possible to start with 31.♗e4, but the text-move was tempting.

31...♗e7 The only move.

32.♗e4

I couldn't find a way to make 32.c7 work, as Black is in time to avert immediate disaster. My training was too human, as I first wanted to put the bishop into play and only then play ♘f3.

'I learned this from Karpov, who was a master in these slow prophylactic moves. In a winning position, in which your opponent cannot move, you simply make useful moves and let your opponent lose the game.'

My move was good enough, but the computer points out that the immediate 32.♘f3 was even stronger: 32...♖d8 33.e3, and there is nothing Black can do against my knight getting to d4, the key square in this position: 33...♗b4 34.♖c1 ♖c7 35.♘d4 ♗a6, and Black's position is bad, although he can still fight.

32...f6

Missing the idea behind 32.♗e4, which is my next move. The best move was 32...♖c8, but he probably didn't like 33.♗d3, which I fully understand, because after 33...♗xd3 34.♘xd3 ♖a6 35.♖ac2 it should be a quite simple technical win. It's very similar to the rook endgame mentioned after move 30, but I like to keep my knight against bishop.

33.♘f3 This is very powerful.

33...♖d8 34.e3

Now the game is practically over.

34...e5

An important detail is that after 34...f5 I have the tactic 35.♘d4, and White wins.

35.fxe5 fxe5

36.♖c1

Another pensioner move. Nothing is threatened, but I like this kind of move. I learned this from Karpov, who was a master in these slow prophylactic moves. In a winning position, in which your opponent cannot move, you simply make useful moves and let your opponent lose the game.

36...a4

Played in desperation. Now, after 36...♗b4, I can already win by force: 37.c7 ♖c8 38.♖ac2 (threatening ♗f5) 38...♗d6 39.♘g5 g6 40.♗d5+ ♔g7 41.♗c6, and because of the knight fork on e6, Black cannot get the pawn on c7, so the game is over.

37.bxa4

And Anish resigned in view of 37...♖xa4 38.♖xa4 ♗xa4 39.c7 ♖c8 40.♗f5.

To my mind, I didn't do that much special in this game, but it received great praise from several Internet commentators. I wouldn't rate it so highly, but then, it's a matter of taste, and who am I to argue with chess specialists? Now it's up to the readers to make up their mind about this game. It was a good game on my part and certainly an important one from a sporting point of view. That's for sure.

∎ ∎ ∎

Kramnik's win allowed two players to draw closer to the leaders. With two rounds to go, Chinese prodigy Yu Yangyi and Arab GM Salem were only half a point behind. Yet if you asked anyone who they thought would win the first Qatar Masters, the vast majority would have told you either Kramnik or Giri. The biggest surprise of the event was still to come. Former Junior World Champion Yu Yangyi had been efficiently lying low and waiting for his chance. In the penultimate round, he inflicted Anish Giri's second consecutive defeat (after six wins!), grinding him down in a marathon game. Giri got a difficult position from the opening and could have lost more quickly.

Former Junior World Champion Yu Yangyi had been efficiently lying low and waiting for his chance. In the penultimate round he ground down Anish Giri in a marathon game.

Giri – Yu Yangyi
Doha 2014 (8)
position after 43.♗xe1

43...♘a4
This keeps a clear advantage, but Black could have finished things off spectacularly with 43...♕b7+! 44.♔h2 (44.♔g1 ♕f3 is the suggestion of my silicon friend. White is dominated by the synergy of the queen-and-knight duo: after 45.♕xc3 ♘d3! Black is going to grab the h3/g4-pawns, after which many mating ideas will follow) 44...♘d1!!, followed by ...♕b2 and ...c2, White cannot prevent Black from queening the c-pawn.
44.d5 ♕d4 45.d6 ♘c5
Yu regards the endgame that has arisen as good enough. Objectively better was 45...♔f8! 46.♗f2 ♕c4, after which it's hard for White to make a move, whilst Black is planning to play ...g6 and ...♔e8, trying to pick up the d6-pawn.
46.♕xc3 ♕xd6 47.♕f3

And as if it wasn't enough, the real torture is starting here!
Objectively speaking this position should be tenable, but Black can keep trying for as long as he wishes. White is struggling, as he can hardly force any further simplifications.

position after 86...♘c3

Fast forward to move 87. Not too much has changed, but now Anish understandably gets impatient.
87.♗xh6?? ♕h2!
87...gxh6? 88.♕e8+ is a perpetual.
88.♕e8+ ♔h7!
And Black escapes from the checks, after which he will win the two remaining white pawns.
89.♗xg7
89.♗f4 won't save White either: 89...♕xh3+ 90.♔g3 ♕h1 91.♔e3 ♕g1+ 92.♔d2 ♕d4+ 93.♔c2 ♕xg4, and Black wins the pawn again.
89...♕h1+ 90.♔f2 ♘e4+ 91.♔e2 ♕g2+

And White resigned in view of 92.♔e3 ♕f2+ 93.♔xe4 ♕e2+, picking up the queen.

Going into the final round, Kramnik was still half a point ahead when he faced Yu Yangyi with the black pieces. After losing his second game Anish was out of contention for first place, but being the fanatic that he is, that didn't stop him from wanting to 'win just one game in a row' and finish the tournament on a positive note. Here's that game with Anish Giri's comments.

NOTES BY
Anish Giri

SI 40.2 – B48
Vladimir Akopian
Anish Giri
Doha 2014 (9)

Believe it or not, I played many decent games in the sunny city of Doha, starting the tournament with six wins, but it is my last-round win that I am really proud of. Although this was far from a clean victory (this is not an understatement), I managed to come back after two consecutive losses to end the tournament on a high note and get my share of the second prize.

1.e4
My opponent, the experienced Armenian grandmaster Vladimir Akopian, is a player with a very healthy understanding of chess. Therefore, I felt obliged to try and complicate matters as quickly as possible. Which explains my choice of the following move:
1...c5 2.♘f3 e6 3.d4 cxd4 4.♘xd4 ♘c6

I have a love-hate relationship with the Taimanov Variation. I lost a painful game with it to Karjakin in the recent Grand Prix tournament in Tashkent, but I've won my share of scalps with it as well.
5.♘c3 ♕c7 6.♗e3
The sharp English Attack, which is introduced with this and the following moves, didn't come as a surprise to me and was obviously quite welcome.

6...a6 7.♕d2 ♘f6 8.0-0-0 ♗b4
This is the old main line, with which I hoped to surprise my opponent. Lately people, myself included, have been more into the fashionable 8...♗e7.
9.f3 ♘e5 10.♘b3
Thousands of games have started from this position. This move is aimed against ...♗xc3, as the e3-bishop is ready to get to the a3-f8 diagonal if given a chance.

10...b5 11.♔b1
Another main move is 11.♕e1. Both moves threaten the well-known, yet painfully nasty trick 12.♘xb5!.
11...♗e7
Avoiding the above-mentioned

cheapo. Another main move is 11...♘c4, which changes the pawn structure once and for all after 12.♗xc4 bxc4.
12.♕f2

One more standard move, preparing g4, while at the same time creating the ♗b6 motif to cause some disharmony on Black's queenside.
12...♗b7!?
A very strong new idea, which I had found just the evening before the game. I had obviously looked at this variation before, but when I started preparing I disliked my original intention and quite quickly stumbled upon this peculiar idea. Before I knew it, I had spotted a couple of coffeehouse tricks and, childish as this may sound, I decided that I must play this variation, if only for the slim chance of catching my experienced opponent in one of those traps. As fate had it, I did catch him, but there was a lot more to it than I had initially thought...
13.♗b6
The standard idea. 13.g4? b4! 14.♘a4 ♘xf3! is cheapo numero uno.
13...♕b8

14.♗d4

14.♗xb5? got me sweating during the game, as I had not thought of it during my preparation, but fortunately there is a strong reply: 14... axb5 15.♘xb5 ♗xe4! 16.♘c7+ (16. fxe4 0-0!) 16...♔f8 17.fxe4 ♖a4!.

14...d6!

This move is the actual novelty, but the entire idea starting with 12...♗b7!? is practically new. There is no need to explain the subtleties of my move order, as its main idea actually happened in the game.

15.g4

What can be more natural? The clever 15.♖g1!? had already been played in this position (reached via a different move order) in Lutz-Perunovic, 2004. Clever as it is, the knight will still be vulnerable on a4: 15...0-0 (a new move) 16.g4 b4 17.♘a4 ♘fd7 (threatening ...♗c6) 18.f4 ♘g6! 19.f5 ♘ge5, and the e4-pawn is hanging and ...♗c6 remains in the position. It is very messy.

15...b4

Once again a very precise move. It's all aimed at one trick...

16.♘a4!?

When I came back to the board and

saw this move, I felt a rather pleasant sensation. Unfortunately, this euphoric state didn't last long, as things turned out to be far more complicated than I had thought.

The alternative was 16.♘e2, but then Black has the easy and very strong plan of pushing his a-pawn.

16...♘xf3!

Blitzed out, obviously!

17.♕xf3!

I had no doubt that my opponent had anticipated my trick, as he had spent quite a lot of time thinking here, and he had managed to come up with something devilish that I hadn't foreseen in my preparation. I had been misled by the computer's assessment, but from a human point of view it is also hard to foresee that White has anything in return for a full exchange and two pawns.

17...♗xe4 18.♕h3 ♗xh1 19.g5

Only here did I realize what was coming. At first I thought, OK, well done, good try. But let me have a think and

the game will be over. However, the deeper I delved into the position, the more problems I found for Black. Finally I settled on what I thought was a reasonably harmonious way of dealing with my uncoordinated pieces, while keeping my material advantage.

19...♘e4

The most natural and most ambitious move.

19...♗c6 would be excellent if White were forced to capture the knight. But he isn't: 20.♘b6! ♘d7 21.♘xa8 e5 22.♘b6 exd4 23.♘c4, with more or less equal material and a balanced position.

After 19...♘d5!? the knight is better positioned in case of g6, but here the problem is the trivial 20.♗xg7! ♘f4 21.♕h4 ♖g8 22.♕xh7 ♖xg7 23.♕xg7 ♗c6.

ANALYSIS DIAGRAM

The attack seems to have been more or less repelled, but actually it hasn't at all: 24.♖d4! e5 25.♖xf4! exf4 26.g6, and the insane complications will eventually lead to perpetual check, which always happens when you switch on a computer in a crazy position.

20.g6! The point. 20.♗xg7 ♘f2 is not what White was aiming for.

20...f6?

Here I was at another gigantic crossroads. I spent my time (about half an hour) quite well. I saw many good variations and found problems with all of the alternatives. After a considerable time weighing the pros and cons I finally settled on this move, which I was very proud of, but which rather unfortunately is a losing mistake.

The most natural and possibly the best move was 20...♘g5, but the problem was that the knight on g5 is constantly in danger of being trapped after a possible h4!: 21.gxf7+ ♔xf7, and the queen can drop to either g3 or e3, with the same idea of h4!, trapping the poor knight on g5. This wasn't clear and I didn't think the position was bad for Black (it seems to be more or less balanced), but it didn't look like a nice position to have to play either.

21.♕xe6? Funnily enough, we both thought this was practically the only move. Instead, White had two alternatives, both of them better than the text, and one simply winning!

21.♗d3!? allows 21...♘g5 but that's not the end of the story: 22.♕e3 ♗f3 23.♖g1! threatening to take on g5 (plus the good old h2-h4), with a very strong attack. Black is on the edge here.

But 21.♗e3!! is the killer. The main idea is simple: White prevents the key idea, ...♘g5. As a bonus, the d4-square is now free for the knight to hop onto: 21...f5 (the best attempt) 22.♘d4!

22...d5 (what else?), and now White can just pick up the h1-bishop, 23.♗d3, with a completely winning position. He will win a full piece, winning back all the lost material, and the attack is yet to start.

21...♘g5 22.♕e3 hxg6!

This was the position I was aiming for. I very much liked the fact that the knight has an excellent outpost on g5 now, thanks to the open h-file. The h8-rook is also participating in the play without having made a single move yet. Yet the position is still far from clear and White has enough compensation. Black has a very weak king and his camp is full of weak squares.

23.♘b6 ♖a7 There were alterna-

tives, but I decided to stay greedy. 23...♖xh2 is anyway met by 24.♗d3!.

24.♗d3 ♖xh2 24...♖h3!? didn't appeal to me, as I was looking forward to eliminating the h-pawn once and for all, but 25.♗xg6+ ♔f8 26.♕f4 ♗c6 is unclear.

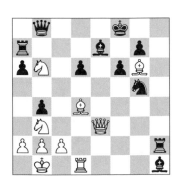

25.♗xg6+?!

It is tempting to grab the pawn with check, but in hindsight White should have started thinking about his next move already here.

Stronger was 25.♘c5!!. Now I would actually be practically forced to take the knight: 25...dxc5 (both 25...♔f7 26.♗c4+ ♔e8 27.♘e6 ♗e4! and 25...f5 26.♘e6 ♘f3 hold, according to the computer, but first of all I don't believe it and secondly, even if it is true, it's not something that you seriously consider in a practical game) 26.♗xg6+ ♔f8, and for my story on this position, see the annotations further down (comments to 26...dxc5).

25...♔f8

26.♘c5!!

A beautiful shot and a very strong one, too. I saw this idea, but it took me a while to believe that it would actually work.

Game over. Anish Giri and Vladimir Akopian briefly check if White could have defended more tenaciously. In the middle Indian GM Abhijeet Gupta and arbiter Ashot Vardapetyan.

time maintaining the tension. It wasn't easy to calculate the variations in this very unbalanced position, but I felt that my opponent's task was even more difficult. He was also getting quite low on time.

30.♖e1? This move pretty much loses, but in time-trouble we both missed quite some details.

30.♖g1! ♖h6 31.♗e3 would keep the game going. Black runs no risk here, but it's hard to make progress with White having excellent pieces and Black being somewhat tied up.

30...♕d8? 30...♕b7! was very precise. I saw this idea, but I didn't see the second intermezzo: 31.♗e4 (31.♗c4 ♖xc4!) 31...♗f7! 32.♕f5, and now 32...♖h5! gives back the exchange and basically takes the game into a winning endgame: 33.♕xh5 ♗xh5 34.♗xb7 ♖xb7 35.♘c8 ♗d8.

31.♘d5 ♗f7 It was tempting to sacrifice back the exchange in this good version, but obviously my opponent would have none of it.

32.♕e4! 32.♘xc7 ♕xc7 is what we call an 'equal plus'.

32...♖d7

33.♘f4?

26...♗c6! The simplest and best solution. Now it slowly transpires that Black has survived the first assault.

26...♔g8!? was also possible, as my opponent pointed out. White has plenty of options and full compensation here.

I used a lot of time calculating 26...dxc5 27.♗xc5

ANALYSIS DIAGRAM

27...♔g8! (I had underestimated this idea. 27...♗f3?? at once seemed winning at first, but here it dawned on me that there is 28.♕f4!! ♕xf4 29.♖d8 mate, ouch) 28.♗xe7, and only now 28...♗f3!. Now White has to show some mathematical precision to hold the balance: 29.♗d6! ♕xd6 30.♖xd6 ♖h1+ 31.♕c1 ♖xc1+ 32.♔xc1 ♘f7 33.♖d4, and White should hold this endgame thanks to his potential counterplay on the queenside.

27.♘e6+ ♘xe6 28.♕xe6 ♗e8 29.♗d3! Keeping the tension. Now it was clear to both of us that Black had repelled the attack, but it was equally clear that White still had quite some compensation.

29...♖c7!? Defending against the threat of 30.♗c4, while at the same

Now my pieces finally get some breathing space, and the game enters the conversion phase, although we were still in time-trouble. My opponent suggested the strong waiting move 33.b3!. White has great positional compensation, which is enough to stay in the game. No variations come to mind, but most importantly, Black can't free himself and it becomes a bit of a waiting game.

33...d5! 34.♘g6+ ♗xg6 35.♕xg6 ♖h6 36.♕g2 ♗d6 37.♖g1 ♖h4?!
A little speculative, but it doesn't spoil too much. However, 37...♕e7!, taking the e-file and preparing ...♗c5, would have been classier.

38.♕xd5? Hoping for a miracle. 38.♗f2! was the right way to give the piece: 38...♖h2 39.♕xd5, and here I would have gone 39...g5! when Black's king will be safe on g7 and I believe Black should eventually win.
38...♗e7! 39.♕g2 ♖dxd4
39...g5!? is more prosaic.
40.♕xg7+ ♔e8 Obviously there is no mate, as White has run out of attacking units. The rest is easy, especially since extra time was added, which was needed to calm down a little.

41.♕g6+ ♔d7 42.♕f5+ ♔c7 43.♕a5+ ♔b8 44.♕xa6 ♖d6 45.♕a4 ♕b6

Black has completely consolidated and enjoys the advantage of an extra rook.
46.♖e1 ♖g4 47.b3 ♖g1 48.♗f1 ♖d8 49.a3 ♗f8 50.♔a2 ♕c5 51.axb4 ♕xb4 52.♕a6 ♖g5 53.♔b2 ♖a5 White resigned.
A pleasing win and a pretty important one. During the game I assumed it wasn't all that perfect, but when I learnt afterwards that at some point I was basically losing in one move... Well, anyway.

■ ■ ■

Your reporter wasn't expecting further last-round excitement. Since Yu Yangyi is a pure 1.e4 player and Kramnik has such a strong Berlin Wall at his disposal, it seemed to me that Kramnik would hold easily and take home the title. A plausible finish to a good tournament for the Russian top GM, right? But Yu Yangyi had a different scenario in mind. Here is what must be the Chinese's favourite game in his career so far, with his own notes.

NOTES BY
Yu Yangyi

RL 7.1 – C65
Yu Yangyi
Vladimir Kramnik
Doha 2014 (9)

Going into the last round, Kramnik was leading the field with 7 out of 8. After defeating Giri in Round 8, I had 6½ points. My previous game had lasted five and a half hours, which cost me a lot of energy. However, I was still excited about playing Kramnik. After all, I grew up studying his games!
1.e4 e5 2.♘f3 ♘c6 3.♗b5 ♘f6 4.d3 ♗c5 5.♗xc6 dxc6 6.♘bd2 ♗e6 7.0-0 ♘d7 8.♘b3 ♗b6!?
I had put more hours into the 8...♗e7 variation. This line is a bit less familiar to me.

9.♘g5 ♗xb3 10.axb3 f6 11.♘f3 ♘f8 12.♘d2 I came up with this move during the game. At the board I thought that White was slightly better after this move. **12...♘e6 13.♕h5+**

With the idea of forcing Black to push ...g6. Then I push f4, and after the

Doha 2014

1	Yu Yangyi	CHN	2705	7½	2905
2	Anish Giri	NED	2776	7	2870
3	Vladimir Kramnik	RUS	2760	7	2829
4	Sanan Sjugirov	RUS	2673	6½	2774
5	Vasif Durarbayli	AZE	2621	6½	2734
6	Zahar Efimenko	UKR	2644	6½	2733
7	Salem A.R. Saleh	UAE	2586	6	2775
8	Andrei Volokitin	UKR	2627	6	2753
9	Maxime Vachier-Lagrave	FRA	2751	6	2743
10	Evgeny Tomashevsky	RUS	2714	6	2734
11	Samuel Shankland	USA	2642	6	2732
12	Milos Perunovic	SRB	2619	6	2727
13	Pavel Eljanov	UKR	2719	6	2725
14	Ivan Ivanisevic	SRB	2643	6	2723
15	Bu Xiangzhi	CHN	2707	6	2720
16	Alexander Moiseenko	UKR	2701	6	2719
17	Ding Liren	CHN	2730	6	2718
18	Eltaj Safarli	AZE	2628	6	2694
19	Sergei Movsesian	ARM	2659	6	2692
20	Vladimir Akopian	ARM	2657	6	2684
21	Ivan Lopez Salgado	ESP	2622	6	2669
22	Baadur Jobava	GEO	2722	6	2664
23	Andrey Vovk	UKR	2640	6	2654
24	Baskaran Adhiban	IND	2630	6	2612
25	Nils Grandelius	SWE	2573	5½	2728
26	Mikhailo Oleksienko	UKR	2620	5½	2719
27	Bela Khotenashvili	GEO	2504	5½	2716
28	Shakhriyar Mamedyarov	AZE	2757	5½	2698
29	Yury Kryvoruchko	UKR	2706	5½	2690
30	Pentala Harikrishna	IND	2725	5½	2689
31	Matthieu Cornette	FRA	2566	5½	2686
32	Daniel Naroditsky	USA	2620	5½	2679
33	Ivan Cheparinov	BUL	2684	5½	2658
34	Evgeny Romanov	RUS	2636	5½	2630
35	Hrant Melkumyan	ARM	2678	5½	2630
36	Rauf Mamedov	AZE	2652	5½	2626
37	Kamil Miton	POL	2601	5½	2621
38	Ferenc Berkes	HUN	2669	5½	2599
39	Alexander Rakhmanov	RUS	2636	5½	2580
40	Hovhannes Gabuzyan	ARM	2565	5½	2570
41	Dariusz Swiercz	POL	2616	5½	2550
42	Kidambi Sundararajan	IND	2415	5½	2549
43	Hicham Hamdouchi	FRA	2616	5½	2542
44	Bogdan Belyakov	RUS	2456	5	2675
45	Gadir Guseinov	AZE	2592	5	2655
46	Robin van Kampen	NED	2612	5	2648
47	Das Debashis	IND	2485	5	2646
48	Abhijeet Gupta	IND	2632	5	2638
154 players, 9 rounds					

exchange on f4, Black's f6-pawn will be weak. Since Black also has doubled pawns on the queenside, White would have quite an enduring advantage!
13...g6 14.♕d1 ♗c5 15.♘c4

15...b5?! This is not a good move, as it allows my knight to enter Black's queenside via a5 and cause problems on c6 and c7.
Better was 15...♕e7 16.♔h1, for example 16...a6 17.f4 exf4 18.♗xf4 ♘xf4 19.♖xf4 0-0-0 20.c3, with a white edge.
16.♘a5 ♕d7 17.♗e3 ♗b6
The alternative was 17...♗d6 18.g3 c5 19.f4 exf4 20.gxf4 0-0 21.♔h1, with a white plus.
18.b4 0-0 19.♕d2

19...f5?! A risky decision. I had expected 19...c5, when after 20.bxc5 ♘xc5 21.b4 ♘e6 22.♘b3 White maintains an edge.
20.exf5 gxf5 21.♕c3

21...f4
I had spent a lot of time thinking about my 21st move. I thought Black would go for 21...♗xa5 22.♖xa5 f4 23.♗xa7 f3 24.♕xe5 ♘f4 25.♕g5+ and I had calculated that far, assuming it was perpetual check. But I had missed that after 25...♔h8 White has 26.♗e3! with a large advantage.
22.♗xb6 cxb6
After 22...axb6 23.♘xc6 would yield White a clear advantage.
23.♘xc6!
After 23.♕xc6 Black has the strong 23...♕c8!.

23...♕d6
I had not seen this move, but after calculating the following sequence I saw that I would be able to meet 25...♘d4 with 26.♘xb5!. I think my opponent made a miscalculation and I grabbed my chance!
Pushing the f-pawn looks attractive, but after 23...f3 there is 24.♘xe5 ♕d5 25.♘xf3 ♖xf3 26.gxf3 ♘d4 27.♕c7!

ANALYSIS DIAGRAM

and White is winning, for example 27...♘e2+ (or 27...♔h8 28.♖fe1 ♘xf3+ 29.♔f1 ♘xe1 30.♔xe1 ♕h1+ 31.♔d2 ♕xa1 32.♕e5+ ♔g8 33.♕d5+, and wins) 28.♔g2 ♔h8 29.♖fe1.

24.♖xa7 ♖xa7 24...f3 loses to 25.♘e7+ ♔h8, and the elegant 26.♘f5.
25.♘xa7 f3 As mentioned above, 25...♘d4 fails to 26.♘xb5 here.

26.♕c6

A good practical choice. I knew my position was winning, but I also realized that I would have to avoid ...♘d4 and possible knight forks.
26...♕e7 27.♘xb5

27...♔h8?! With 27...fxg2 Black would at least have got some counterplay, although he could still be lost after 28.♔xg2 ♔h8 29.♔h1.
28.g3

After this move I was pretty sure that I was winning, because I had seen the effective plan ♖a1, followed by ♖a8, when I would be three pawns up after the rook swap.
28...♕f7 29.♖a1 ♘g5 30.♖a8 ♕e7 31.h4 ♘h3+ 32.♔f1 e4

32...♕xb4 ends the game immediately, as it allows the blow 33.♕f6+.
33.♕xe4 Black resigned.
I was very happy about defeating my opponent and winning the tournament. But I was also exhausted and in need of a good rest!

■ ■ ■

Former World Champion meets former Junior World Champion. Yu Yangyi: 'My previous game had lasted five and a half hours, which cost me a lot of energy. However, I was still excited about playing Kramnik. After all, I grew up studying his games!'

And so the contest in Doha came to a thrilling end with the strong-willed Yu Yangyi reeling in the point. After the two top favourites had both treated the fans to amazing six-win streaks, who could have thought that anyone else than either of them would steal the show?

After playing a major role in China's victory at the Olympiad in Tromsø, Yu Yangyi has now shown that he is ready for bigger things in individual tournaments. His strong nerves, terrific opening preparation and willingness to play long and hard-fought games make him a formidable candidate to join the absolute elite in the near future.

Of course, Anish Giri and Vladimir Kramnik can look back on Qatar with positive feelings, too. As heart-breaking as it can be to lose one of the final games, both players managed to display dominating chess and showed their class when playing second-tier grandmasters.

The short-lived headlines of Big Vlad dropping out of the Top 10 in the Live Ratings were rectified after his performance in Doha, and I doubt that we'll see him fall off again in 2015. Looking at his games in Qatar, the only critical remarks are evoked by his overly creative play in his first two games. But then again, it seems nothing less than healthy to me that the former World Champion occasionally enjoys himself, moving from endless Catalans to making moves like g4 as early as move 7!

As for my friend Anish, I'll be happy to see him enter the Top 10 at the end of this year. Even though his streak of losses against certain players is yet to come to an end, he seems to be improving his game steadily. At the same time, if it's not me who is going to make him worry about players of his own age catching up, I'm glad there are others to remind him that it won't only be Magnus he will still have to cope with in the coming years.

To conclude, I'd like to render my thanks to GM Al-Modiahki, who has managed to organize a highly exciting event. As for the future of the Qatar Masters, let's just say that it's highly doubtful that I'll ever make it to the Top 10 seeds in that flashy event in the Middle East ☺. ■

For a man with a chronic addiction to exotic travel, the prospect of participating in the Myanmar International Open, in November, was simply impossible to resist. An additional inducement was the notion of partly retracing the footsteps of my grandfather Jack, who had played his small part in the extensive campaigns against the Japanese in the Burmese jungle under General Slim. The fighting was extremely bitter, went on for years, and left an otherwise gentle man with an abiding hatred for 'the enemy'. Incidentally, on a melancholy family note, the only time my father ever witnessed his parents embrace was at the front door when Jack eventually returned to England.

Alas, shortly after the tournament was announced, Zaw Win Lay – Myanmar's solitary grandmaster – died from the effects of diabetes and high blood-pressure in Mandalay at the relatively young age of 51. The tournament was duly renamed in his honour. When I played him in the Thailand Open, as recently as 2011, he looked fine. I could never have imagined he would depart life so soon. Who knows when our time is up?

Myanmar is opening up rapidly to both business and tourism, but after decades of groaning under the yoke of a military dictatorship, Yangon – the principal city – is still far from being an international hub. The most convenient way for me to travel there was via neighbouring Bangkok, where Kai Tuorila, the energetic organiser of the Thailand Open, had inveigled me into participating in one of his club's regular blitz tournaments. By chance, Petri Deryng, a fellow Finn and one of the main sponsors of the international open, was marrying his gorgeous girlfriend Ning and kindly invited me to a grand reception at the Royal Bangkok Sports Club. I thus had two excellent reasons to stay for a couple of days – not that I needed much persuasion to acclimatise in that most vibrant of oriental capitals. The 9-round FIDE-rated blitz event at the Queen Victoria pub served as a useful barometer of my form. The modest field was bolstered slightly by other foreigners who were similarly en route, but as top seed by a country-mile, I should have won comfortably. A headache, caused by the twin afflictions of jet-lag and dehydration, contributed to me losing two completely winning positions, and I could only finish in second place. As an inexperienced Mikhail Botvinnik discov-

Burmese Days

ered, when he arrived just two hours before the start of the first round at Hastings 1934/35, one can't just show up after an exhausting journey and expect to perform well immediately – no matter how strong you are. Thankfully, I still had a couple of days to recover.

I was greeted at Yangon airport by my old friend, the chief arbiter Peter Long from Malaysia, and by Maung Maung Lwin – the President of the Myanmar Federation, who drove us to the 3-star Central Hotel downtown. Labour in Burma is abundant and cheap, but decent accommodation is rather pricey, due to the recent spike in demand and an acute shortage of supply. The conveniently situated hotel, which doubled as the venue, was perfectly adequate, apart from the dodgy Internet, but by no means luxurious.

As the next day was free, we took the opportunity for a little sightseeing. The extraordinary 99 metre tall, gilded Shwedagon Pagoda, set in a vast ancient religious complex, with its anachronistic escalators and ATMs (kudos for not disguising the racket), was the first port of call. Unfortunately it was undergoing repair and could not be seen in its full resplendent glory, but even in these less flattering circumstances it was an awe-inspiring sight. After such a climax, other attractions – such as the Nga Htat Gyi Buddha, or the huge indoor Scott Market with its jade and jewelry – were almost disappointing in comparison.

The playing field was comprised of 10 GMs headed by fellow traveller Sergey Tiviakov down to Serbian journeyman Stefan Djuric, assorted other title-holders and a substantial tail of mostly local unrated participants. The latter group was a very mixed bag: some could play and some could not. While egalitarianism may sound fine in principle, 50 or 60 of these hopefuls could and probably should have been packed off to a separate event.

One day we will get a wise FIDE President who will justly decree that tournaments with double rounds cannot under any circumstances be Elo-rated, but until such time we will have to endure inhumane schedules (rectifying this would be a productive use of ACP President Emil Sutovsky's abundant misplaced energy). The Zaw Win Lay Memorial, alas, began with three consecutive days of immense cruelty. True, the first round was not too taxing (Tiviakov, for one, removed his opponent's pieces at very regular intervals), but these games still had to be played and were a drain. The 9 a.m. start did not suit everyone either. Like any parent, I am accustomed to rising early, so it doesn't bother me that much – although clearly opening preparation has to be sharply curtailed or even abandoned altogether. Also, when Anand's 11th game exchange sacrifice in Sochi backfired, I was urgently required to write a summary of the World Championship match for the Financial Times – a task which was only completed well beyond midnight. Sleep inevitably suffered as a consequence.

One of the nicest things about this event was being regally entertained by Maung Maung Lwin each evening. We would typically head off to some restaurant called 'Golden Duck', or 'Junior Duck' by the banks of the Irrawaddy and feast upon canard, fish and vegetables – although probably the best culinary experience was at a more distant establishment, specialising in Burmese cuisine. In contrast to the loquacious Peter Long, he is a fairly taciturn individual, but slowly, over the course of several days, a fuller picture of this unassuming character would emerge. Unlike many a FIDE official, he is deeply passionate about chess. At a time when literature was hard to come by in this closed society, he copied out over 50 books by hand – displaying a dedication that few die-hard fans could even match. After the Tromsø Olympiad, he flew to Reykjavik and thence continued somewhat expensively by taxi to Selfoss for the express purpose of seeing Bobby Fischer's grave. I might add that he has also written on the Burmese variant of chess – a version which deserves recognition, respect and indeed preservation.

Your scribe cruised, without too many bumps, to 4/4, but the wheels came off completely on the third day. First, I obtained less than nothing against Arun Prasad in the morning, which was disappointing, but not a calamity. However, in the evening I suffered one of the fastest defeats of my professional career, when I was destroyed in just 20 moves by his compatriot, MR Venkatesh. One could criticise, with some justification, my choice of opening – a sharp Richter-

'Sergey had somehow acquired a huge box of fried grasshoppers and a jar of bamboo worms upon which he was ostentatiously munching while scaring away more sensitive souls.'

Rauzer – with which I was insufficiently familiar (as was my opponent, in fact), but the real problem was that I just could not calculate anything, due to fatigue.

At this point I felt that Tiviakov, who was alone on 5½/6, was red-hot favourite to win. Nevertheless, the rest day throws up temptations, which for Sergey meant indulging his taste for the entomological and repulsive. When I met him in the lobby, he had somehow acquired a huge box of fried grasshoppers and a jar of bamboo worms – a local delicacy, apparently – upon which he was ostentatiously munching while scaring away more sensitive souls. Whether the ingesting of these questionable comestibles adversely affected his performance I know not, but the fact is the next day he barely survived against the talented but timid 14-year-old Singaporean Tin Jingyao, and subsequently he was humbled by Arun Prasad in the following round. This unexpectedly put the Indian in clear first place with one game remaining.

In the meantime, I had sneaked up quietly with a couple of victories and now faced the aggressive Jahongir Vakhidov from Uzbekistan. A win would put me in the money. Preferring breakfast to preparation, I whipped up a dangerous kingside attack from a rather dubious Trompowsky. With success in sight I briefly faltered, but in time-trouble he missed his one chance to escape and I crashed through.

On top board, Prasad appeared incredibly nervous against the Grünfeld of Vladimir Belous – at 2578 the third seed. Nevertheless, he outplayed the Russian, before overlooking a forced win. He eventually stumbled into an endgame where his two bishops were unable to halt Black's rook and pawns. This meant Belous (who won his last 4 games) and I shared first place.

The tournament, which was sponsored by the Kasparov Chess Foundation and attended by the Minister for Sport, attracted plenty of TV and other media. Maung intends it to become an annual event. If he goes ahead as planned and eases the schedule for 2015, I wouldn't be at all surprised to see it gaining in popularity and increasing in strength. For those of a somewhat adventurous disposition, Yangon has plenty to offer. ∎

Quick, quick, slow

6th London Chess Classic embraces all rated time-controls

When the London Classic switched from classical chess to rapid play last year, it created a tournament which was very exciting but bestrewn with errors. The return to classical chess in the 6th edition was therefore greeted with considerable approbation by many, including our reporter **Jonathan Speelman**. But the six-player tournament was appreciably smaller than previous editions, and while it was excellent, it was at the very least no more dramatic than the huge rapid-play which preceded it – or the blitz tournament that served as the drawing of lots for the main event.

The 'Super Rapidplay Open' included all six players in the Classic itself, another 28 GMs and about 40 IMs. This by itself was more than enough for a very tough tour, but the field in total comprised over 400 players, the bottom 300 or so rated 2200 or lower. With such a long and juicy tail, it was no great surprise that six players made a perfect 5/5 on the first day and that the top seed Hikaru Nakamura was among them.

There had been a number of scares along the way, though, and Nakamura himself had lost a whole piece for a single pawn as early as move 11 against English IM James Adair in Round 4, although he then somehow contrived not only to draw but even win.

RAY MORRIS-HILL

Nakamura was under pressure against Matthew Sadler in the first game of the second day, but wriggled out to a draw and thereafter he was imperious, defeating Michael Adams, Anish Giri, Fabiano Caruana and Vishy Anand on the trot, garnering an incredible 9½/10. Giri was second on 8½ and 10 players on 8: Caruana, Anand, Vladimir Kramnik, Nigel Short, Alex Lenderman, Eric Hansen, Daniel Naroditsky, Alon Greenfeld, Nick Pert and Simon Williams.

A few moves earlier, Anand could have simply exchanged knight for bishop, but he wanted to keep the tension, since he was half a point behind. 28...g5 should still be fine, since if 29.♖c7 ♖d2+ 30.♔e1 ♖b2 31.♖xa7 ♘f5 32.♖cc7 ♖b1+ is just a perpetual, but Anand went pawn hunting and it soon went horribly wrong.
28...♖h5 29.♖c7 ♖xh2
29...a5 was much better, but the position was already most uncomfortable.
30.♖xa7 ♘d5 31.a5! bxa5 32.bxa5 ♖h5 33.♖b7

With so many games, there were lots of interesting tactical interludes, including this one.

McShane-Agdestein
London rapid 2014 (7)
position after 27...♕xe8

McShane had just exchanged rooks on e8 and now captured:
28.♘xd4
It looks as though the tactics are fine for White and Luke will certainly have been ready for example for 28...♕h5

Nakamura-Anand
London rapid 2014 (10)
position after 28.a4

The huge passed a-pawn now wins a piece and White won easily.

29.♘f3. Agdestein replied **28...♘e5** and later lost.

But White's pieces are loose on the d-file and it turns out that this can be exploited.

If 28...♕d7? 29.♕f5! unravels (and, indeed, 29.♕b5 is quite good, too). But 28...♕d8!! wins material – a stroke that a machine sees in milliseconds but a strong player could quite conceivably miss even in a classical game. Of course, if 29.♘xc6 (or anywhere else) then 29...♗xh2+!, and 29.♗e3 or 29.♗c3 will be met by 29...♗c5. The best White can do is 29.♕e4 ♘xd4 30.♗xh6, but the simple 30...♗c5 should win in the long run.

8/10 means an uphill battle to win a prize and my impression was that you either had to have a stellar ambient level, like Nakamura and the other top guys, or had to be lucky – or at the very least not unlucky – and, even more importantly, young.

The older guys were able to perform for a while, but cracked up later. I personally had a really good first day, but a distinctly average second one, and made 7/10. While John Nunn, for example, won his first three games on both days but then subsided to the extent that he also made 'just' 7.

Whinging aside, it was a wonderful tournament on a scale I can't recall in London for many years, if at all. Malcolm Pein deserves huge credit for shoe-horning it before the Classic. There were many nice touches, such as the guarantees he offered to people like myself without even being asked. He himself even found time to partic-

ipate in the fun – though unsurprisingly he couldn't play in every round – and finished on 6½/10 (5/6 and three half-point byes).

Since it was introduced a few years ago at the Tal Memorial in Moscow, a preliminary blitz tournament to decide the pairings for the main event has become distinctly trendy. Adams was first on tie-break, ahead of Nakamura and Kramnik. These three obviously chose the top half numbers, which get an extra White [which in

> ## 'Kramnik was flabbergasted when Nigel Short told him that the position after 40 moves had occurred in 10(!) games, all played by computers.'

the end, given the tiebreakers that were used, turned out not to be an advantage at all – ed.].

The first round of a tournament is always particularly important, especially if it's as short as the Classic was. Two of the games featured excellent opening preparation. Particularly Kramnik-Anand saw some ridiculously heavy theory in the Botvinnik Variation of the Slav. Kramnik was flabbergasted when Nigel Short told him that the position after 40 moves had occurred in 10(!) games, all played by computers. 'Well, computers have a lot of time', joked Anand.

The third game of the first round was a riveting and fluctuating struggle, which ended with Adams victorious against Caruana.

RL 19.13 – C90
Michael Adams
Fabiano Caruana
London 2014 (1)

1.e4 e5 2.♘f3 ♘c6 3.♗b5 a6 4.♗a4 ♘f6 5.0-0 ♗e7 6.♖e1 b5 7.♗b3 0-0 8.d3 d6 9.c3 ♘a5 10.♗c2 c5 11.♘bd2 ♘c6 12.♘f1 h6 13.♘e3 ♖e8 14.a4 ♗e6

It was round about here that both players began to think seriously.

15.h3 ♗f8 16.♘h2

16...b4 This move, which puts some pressure on White's queenside, but weakens the light squares, is possibly a novelty.

16...d5 17.axb5 axb5 18.♖xa8 ♕xa8 19.exd5 ♘xd5 20.♘eg4 ♘f4 21.♗f3 was tried in Spraggett-Sargissian, Linares Open 2013, which was eventually drawn.

17.♗b3 ♖b8 18.♗c4 bxc3 19. bxc3

19...d5

Black needs to do something before White arranges to exchange a pair of knights and plant a piece on d5.

20.♗xa6

Exchanging three times on d5 would have left d3 weak, so this makes sense, although the tactics aren't great for White. Which suggests that some earlier move was a little inaccurate.

20...♛a5

21.c4?!
21.♗b5 ♖xb5! 22.axb5 ♛xa1 is a bit better for Black, but this fighting move, while admirable, is worse.
21...♛xa6 22.exd5 ♗xd5 23. cxd5

23...♞b4! Hitting d3 and putting White in trouble.
24.♖a3 ♞fxd5 25.♞eg4 f6 26.♞f1 ♖bd8
It seems that 26...♖ed8 was even better.
27.♞g3

27...c4?

At the traditional closing dinner at Simpson's-in-the-Strand, Nigel Short and David Norwood test a fine Purling chess set watched by commentator Lawrence Trent, Fabiano Caruana and Vishy Anand.

Up to here this game has been all Black, but this hasty move incites White to play a sacrifice that is at least adequate.
28.♞xh6+! gxh6 29.♛g4+ ♚h8

30.dxc4
Because of 27...c4, White has this move, which captures another pawn and affects Black's coordination.
30...♞f4 would have been wise now, but Caruana tried to keep his booty and the rest until move 40 was an increasingly frantic time-scramble. I'll point out one clear win for White during this, but there's not too much point in nit-picking until they had time to think again.
30...♞e7?! 31.♛h5!

31...♞g8? Obvious, but too greedy.
32.♞f5! ♛b7 33.♖g3 ♛h7

34.♞h4
34.♖e4! was winning after 34...♞d3 35.♖eg4 ♞xc1 36.♖xg8+ ♛xg8 37.♖xg8+ ♚xg8 38.♛g6+ ♚h8

39.♘xh6 ♗xh6 40.♕xh6+ ♔g8
41.♕g6+ ♔h8 42.♕xf6+ ♔h7
43.♕f7+ ♔h6 44.g4 ♘e2+ 45.♔h2
♖f8 46.♕h5+ ♔g7 47.♕xe5+.
34...♘e7 35.♗a3
Probably having missed the reply:
35...♘bc6!

36.♔h2!
Recovering his balance, but the next
move helped Black.
**36...♗g7 37.♗xe7? ♘xe7
38.♖d1 ♕g8 39.♖b1 ♖b8 40.♖d1
♖ed8**

And so to the relative calm of move
40. Despite the piece deficit, White's
residual attack and passed pawns are
sufficient for equality.
41.c5 ♖xd1 42.♕xd1 ♖b4?
This looks sensible but allows the
white queen to d7, after which the
pawns become too strong. Instead,
42...♖d8 43.♖d3 ♖xd3 44.♕xd3
♕c8 was correct, when 45.♕d6 ♘f5
46.♘xf5 ♕xf5 47.c6 ♕f4+ is perpetual check.
43.♕d7! ♖xh4 44.♕xe7

White has a cute threat here: to take
twice on g7 and then play 48.g4!!,
immuring the h4-rook and allowing the queenside pawns to promote
without hindrance.
44...♖d4 There's no time to liqui-
date with 44...♕f8, because 45.♖xg7
♕xg7 46.♕xg7+ ♔xg7 47.g4! ♔g6
48.c6 simply wins. While, of course,
if 44...♖xa4 45.♖xg7 ♕xg7 46.♕e8+
plus xa4.
45.c6 The engines say that 45.a5 is
even stronger.

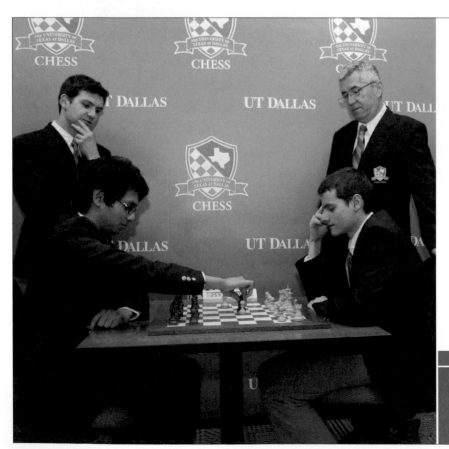

45...♕f8 46.♕b7 ♖b4 47.♕d7 ♖d4 48.♕b7 ♖b4

49.♖c3!
This beautiful move leads to victory.
49...f5 50.♕d7 ♖d4 51.♕e6 ♖d6
If 51...♖d8 then 52.c7 ♖c8 53.a5 e4 54.♖c5 keeps control.
52.♕xd6! ♕xd6 53.c7 e4+ 54.g3 ♗xc3 55.c8♕+ ♔h7 56.♕xc3 f4 57.gxf4 ♕xf4+ 58.♕g3 ♕d2 59.♕c7+ ♔g6 60.♕b6+

After a fine victory in the blitz tournament and the boost of beating Caruana, Michael Adams, the English number one, unfortunately went downhill.

The a-pawn should be too much here. After 60...♔g7! 61.♕c7+ ♔f6 62.♕c5 ♔g6 63.♔g2 there would still have been plenty of work to do, but Caruana dropped the e-pawn with:
60...♔h7? 61.♕b7+ ♔h8 62.♕a8+! ♔g7 63.♕xe4

63...♔f6
Of course, if 63...♕xf2+, the cross check 64.♕g2+ concludes matters.
64.♕f3+ ♔g6 65.♔g2 ♕a2 66.♕e4+ ♔f6 67.♕f4+ ♔g6 68.♕d6+ ♔g7 69.♕e5+ ♔h7 70. a5 ♕g8+ 71.♔h2 ♕f7 72.♕e4+ ♔g7 73.a6 1-0

Rather than bumble through the tournament round by round, it might be better to concentrate on the players, starting with Adams. After a fine victory in the blitz tournament and the boost of beating Caruana, the English number one unfortunately went downhill. Giri squeezed him to death in Round 2, but probably the most critical moment was in Round 3, when Kramnik misplayed a rook ending and for a fleeting moment just before the time control was demonstrably lost.

Adams played a 'safe' move which looked as though it would spoil nothing, but sadly it did and the moment passed and with it his grip on the tournament.

Adams-Kramnik
London 2014 (3)
position after 39...♔d7

40.c5
40.f6! d3 41.♖xd3 ♖xg4 42.e6+ fxe6+ 43.♔e5+ ♔e8 44.♔xe6 ♖e4+ 45.♔f5 ♖xc4 46.♔g6! ♖f4 47.♖e3+ ♔d7 48.f7 should be winning, but in time-pressure Adams's last move before the time-control was a mistake, since he'd missed 42...♖e3!, after which the draw was reasonably straightforward.
40...bxc5 41.♔xc5 ♖e4 42.♔d5 ♖e3 43.♖g2 d3 44.♖d2 ♖g3 45.♖d1 ♖xg4 46.♖xd3 ♖f4 47.f6 ♖f1 48.e6+ ♔e8 49.exf7+ ♔xf7 50.♖c3 ♖f5+ 51.♔c6 g4 52.♖g3 ♖g5 53.♔xc7 ♖xb5 54.♖xg4 ½-½

A single win in the last round, crucially with Black, proved enough for Vishy Anand to win the London Classic on tie-break ahead of Kramnik and Giri.

We'll take the other players from the top downwards, starting with the winner. It's impressive that Vishy Anand could play at all so close to the World Championship, which was hanging over him every time he met anybody, even if they had the decency not to refer to it directly. But he still fought so well in the rapid-play that, had he beaten Nakamura in the final round rather than lost in a bid for glory, he would have been first.

In the Classic he started quite conservatively with the huge screeds of theory against Kramnik and draws with Caruana and Nakamura. He opened up more in the penultimate round against Giri and got a pretty promising position before that, too, was drawn. In the final round, the suffering Adams blew up in the endgame and a single win, crucially with black, proved sufficient for first on tie-break ahead of Kramnik and Giri, in that order.

RL 7.4 – C67
Michael Adams
Vishy Anand
London 2014 (5)

**1.e4 e5 2.♘f3 ♘c6 3.♗b5 ♘f6
4.0-0 ♘xe4 5.d4 ♘d6 6.♗xc6
dxc6 7.dxe5 ♘f5 8.♕xd8+ ♔xd8**

The Berlin Wall has become so ubiquitous at the elite level that of the seven games in London in which White opened 1.e4, Black played the Berlin in five, with four instances of the Wall itself and Nakamura ducking as White against Giri.

It's a line which is both so complicated and outwardly simple that it's a nightmare for commentators and spectators. Nigel Short suggested jocularly, but only just, that players should 'be fined for playing it'. Quizzed about it afterwards, Anand pointed out that the revival had been in the Kasparov-Kramnik World Championship in London in 2000, so perhaps it should be called the London Wall. Rather than get heavily involved, I'm going to go for the main points.

**9.h3 ♔e8 10.♘c3 h5 11.♖d1
♗e7 12.g3 b6 13.a4 ♗b7 14.a5
c5 15.♘d5 ♗d8 16.♗g5 ♖f8**

17.c4 Obvious, but it does weaken d4, perhaps unnecessarily.
17...♗xd5 18.♖xd5
18.cxd5 ♗xg5 19.♘xg5 ♔e7 20.♘f3 f6 is alright for Black.
18...♗xg5

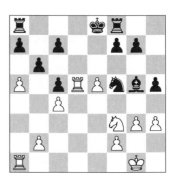

19.♘xg5 The intermezzo 19.axb6! cxb6 would have prevented ...c6 later. Black can try 19...c6, but 20.♖xa7 ♖b8 21.♖dd7 ♗d8 22.♖db7 gives White more than enough for the piece: 22...♖xb7 (22...♖c8? 23.♘d2!) 23.♖xb7 h4 24.g4 ♘d4 25.♔g5 f5 26.exf6 ♖xf6 27.♖b8 ♔e7 28.b7 ♗c7 29.♖c8 ♗e5 30.b8♕ ♗xb8 31.♖xb8, regaining it with some advantage.
**19...♔e7 20.♔g2 ♘d4 21.♖d1
♖ad8 22.♘f3 c6 23.♖xd8 ♖xd8
24.♘g5 b5 25.cxb5 cxb5 26.♘e4
♘c6 27.♖xd8 ♔xd8**

28.e6? A mistake in time-pressure. 28.f4 ♘xa5 29.♘xc5 ♔e7 30.♔f3 is fine for White.
28...fxe6 29.♘xc5 ♔e7 30.♘b3 ♔d6 31.♔f3 ♔d5 32.♔f4 ♘c4 33.♘c1 ♘xa5 34.♔g5 ♘b3 35.♘e2 b4 36.♔xh5 a5

The scramble has been catastrophic for White and, unable to stop the a-pawn, Adams resigned.

After the draw with Anand, Kramnik won a really good game against Nakamura in Round 2. He survived the scare against Adams, drew a complicated battle with Caruana and came fairly close to beating Giri as Black in the final round, which would have given him first.

KI 17.4 – E92
Vladimir Kramnik
Hikaru Nakamura
London 2014 (2)

1.d4 ♘f6 2.c4 g6 3.♘c3 ♗g7 4. e4 d6 5.♗e2 0-0 6.♘f3 e5 7.d5 a5 8.♗g5 h6

9.♗e3 Kramnik has always enjoyed playing against the King's Indian and

indeed it was arguably because of him that Kasparov shied away from the KID later on in his career.

Tigran Petrosian once said that it was 8.♗g5 that put food on his family's table, but of course he played 9.♗h4 rather than this provocative move.
9...♘g4 10.♗d2 f5 11.h3 ♘f6 12. exf5 gxf5 13.♕c1 f4 14.g3 e4 15.♘h4 e3 16.fxe3 fxg3 17.♘g6

Kramnik had been playing very quickly with some preparation which he apparently had done a year or so ago, and now, after some thought, Nakamura decided on:
17...♖f7?!
After 17...♖e8, which looks better, Nakamura didn't like 18.♕c2 ♘a6 19.♘f4 to play 20.♕g6, missing the very strong riposte 19...♖e5!. Kramnik had obviously found a reasonable line against 17...♖e8, but it looks scary for White to me, for example if 18.♕c2 (I imagine that 18.♖g1 may in fact be better) 18...♘a6 19.0-0-0 ♘b4 20.♕b1 ♘e4!, with a large advantage, since Black intends 21.♘xe4 ♗f5!.
18.♕c2 ♘fd7?!

This looks primarily designed to avoid Kramnik's preparation – 18...♘a6 was much more natural.
19.0-0-0

19...♘e5?!
19...♘c5 looks messier. Now Kramnik gets a big lead in development. In the VIP-room there was now a bet between Julian Hodgson and Lawrence Trent as to whether White would play ♖hf1 or ♘h4, which Julian won.

20.♖hf1!
This excellent move exchanges off the f7-rook – a vital defender.
20...♖xf1 21.♖xf1 ♗xh3 22.♖g1 ♕f6 23.♖xg3 ♘xg6 24.♖xg6 ♕f7 25.♖g3 ♗f5 26.e4 ♗g6 27.♗g4

It's all gone horribly wrong for Black. Nakamura now tried to fight his way out, but 27...♔h8 was also awful.
27... ♕f1+ 28.♘d1 ♗e5 29.♗h3! ♕f6 30.♖g1 ♔h7 31.♗f5 ♗xf5 32.exf5 ♘d7 33.♖g6 ♕f7 34.♖xh6+ ♔g8 35.♖g6+ ♔f8

41.gxh5 Very slightly encouraging for Black, since 41.♗xe6 fxe6 42.♕d7+ ♔h6 43.♕xe6+ ♗g6 44.gxh5 ♔xh5 45.♕h3+ ♕h4 46.♕c8 ♗c2 47.♕h8+ ♔g6 48.♕f6+ was an immediate draw.
41...♔h6 42.♕d8 ♕xe5 43.♕f8+ ♔g7 44.♕xg7+ ♔xg7

36.♘f2 Bringing the last piece into the attack. The ever resourceful Nakamura still found a way almost to create problems, but it would have been a travesty if the tactics had not favoured White decisively.
36...b5 37.♘g4 bxc4 38.♕xc4 ♕xf5 39.♖g8+! ♔e7 40.♗g5+ ♗f6 41.♕e2+!
And Nakamura resigned.

Like the previous two, Giri also had a win and four draws, or 7/15 under the football scoring system. His win was in Round 2 against Adams, and one of the most impressive moments was when he defended himself with great accuracy against Kramnik in the final round.

A Catalan had gone seriously wrong for Giri against the world's greatest expert and ...♗c5-d4 was a big threat. But Giri found:
32.♕c4! ♗c5 33.♗e2 ♗d4 34.♗d3!

Challenging the bishop just in time.
34...♕a1!
Making some trouble. If 34...♗xd3 then 35.♕xd3 ♗xb2 36.♕xb3 ♗xe5 is completely equal, but he could have tried 35...♕a4 36.♗c3 ♗xc3 37.♕xc3 ♕xe4+, with some pressure.
35.♕xd4 ♕xe1 36.♗c4 ♗xe4+ 37.f3 ♗c2 38.♗d3+ g6 39.♗c4 g5 40.g4 h5

45.h4 Sensibly simplifying, though 45.♗b5 ♔h6 46.♗e8 f5 was also quite good enough.
45...♔h6 46.hxg5+ ♔xh5 47.♔f2 ♔xg5 48.♔e3 ♔f5 49.f4

Giri-Kramnik
London 2014 (5)
position after 31...♔h7

Despite the extra pawn, Black has absolutely no winning chances, since White can even afford to lose the bishop and f-pawn for the two centre pawns, when ♔ + b2 v ♔, ♗ and b3 is a fortress with the king on c1.

It ended: **49...♔g4 50.♗b5 ♔f5 51.♗c4 ♔g6 52.♔f2 ♔f6 53.♔f3 ♔g6 54.♔f2 ♗d1 55.♔e3 ♔f5 56.♗b5 ♔g4 57.♗e8 f6 58.♗d7 ♔f5 59.♗b5 ♗c2 60.♗d7 ♗b1 61.♗a4 ♗c2 62.♗d7 ♗b1 63.♗a4 ♗c2 ½-½**

After his defeat by Kramnik in Round 2, Hikaru Nakamura bounced back against Adams in an excellent game in Round 4. He was still in with a shout for first before the final round (if the other results went his way) and was pretty close to defeating Caruana at one stage, which would indeed have given him clear first. But after some mistakes he ended up having to defend himself, and indeed, if Caruana had wished, he could probably have forced rook and bishop vs. rook when he was still hoping for more.

QO 16.6 – D30
Hikaru Nakamura
Michael Adams
London 2014 (4)

1.d4 ♘f6 2.c4 e6 3.♘f3 d5 4.♗g5
A little more unusual than 4.♘c3 first.
4...♗e7 5.♕c2 h6 6.♗xf6 ♗xf6 7.e3

7...c5!?
This is certainly what Black wants to play, but the tactics seem to be against him as, I suspect, Nakamura had checked at home at some stage.
8.cxd5 cxd4 9.♗b5+ ♗d7
Both 9...♗e7 and 9...♔f8 were conceivable, for after 9...♗d7 10.dxe6! is annoying.
10.dxe6!

10...♕a5+ If 10...♗xb5 11.exf7+ then if 11...♔xf7 12.♕b3+ or 11...♔e7 (or ...♔f8) 12.♕c5+ immediately regains the piece with interest; while on 11...♔d7 12.♕f5+ ♔c6 13.a4 ♗a6 14.b4 is too strong.
11.♘bd2 ♕xb5 Of course, Black would love to play 11...♗xb5 12.♕c8+ ♔e7 (12...♕d8 13.♕xb7!) 13.♕xh8 ♘d7 14.♕xa8 ♘c5, but sadly it's completely unsound.
12.exd7+ ♘xd7 13.♕e4+ ♔f8 14.♘xd4

14...♕xb2 Also interesting and probably better was 14...♕a6 15.♖c1 ♖e8 16.♕d5, and now, in the VIP room, we looked at:

ANALYSIS DIAGRAM

16...♘e5 17.♖c3! g6 (17...♘d3+?? 18.♖xd3 ♕xd3 19.♘e6+) 18.♖a3!, with a large advantage, but 16...♘b6 is better though: 17.♕c5+ (17.♕b5 ♗xd4 18.♕b4+ ♔g8 19.♕xd4 ♔h7 is a bit scary) 17...♔g8 18.♕b5 (hitting e8) 18...♕xb5 19.♘xb5 ♗xb2 20.♖b1 or possibly 20.♖c7 ♖c8 21.♖xc8+ ♘xc8 22.♔e2 is a safe way to get an edge.
15.♖b1 ♕xa2 16.♕xb7
16.0-0 looks nice and indeed, if 16...♕xd2, then the tactics do work for White: 16...♕xd2? 17.♕xb7 ♖d8 18.♖fd1 ♕a2 19.♘c6 ♘c5 20.♕b8!. But after 16.0-0 ♘c5! 17.♕f5 b6 is okay for Black.

Hikaru Nakamura was pretty close to winning the Classic, but missed his chance in the last round. The American did win the Rapid with an incredible 9½ from 10.

16...♖d8

Nakamura felt quite reasonably that 16...♖b8 17.♕xd7 ♖xb1+ 18.♘xb1 ♕xb1+ 19.♔e2 ♕b2+ (of course not 19...♕xh1?? 20.♕c8+ ♔e7 21.♘f5 mate) 20.♔f3 g6 was the lesser evil, though of course White will always get 4 vs. 3 in one form or another.
17.♕b4+ ♔g8 18.0-0 a5 19.♕c3 ♕d5 20.♕c7 ♘f8 21.♖b5! ♕d7 22.♕xd7 ♖xd7 23.♘2f3

> 'Caruana's form in St. Louis in September was so out of this world that there was bound to be a reaction.'

23...♗xd4 Knights are generally better than bishops in endgames with play only on one flank, so this certainly makes sense.
24.♘xd4 ♘e6 25.♘xe6 fxe6 26.♖xa5 ♔f7

27.g4 This is the move that White wants to play, since if he can get in g4 and h4-h5, then Black is definitely on the brink. White is pretty close, for example, to getting Botvinnik vs. Najdorf, Moscow 1956, in which the diagram is demonstrably winning:

65...♔e7 66.e6 ♖a4 67.g5 hxg5 68.♖d7+ ♔f8 69.♖f7+ ♔g8 70.♔g6 g4 71.h6 gxh6 72.e7 ♖a8 73.♖f6 1-0. Back to Nakamura-Adams, after 27.g4,

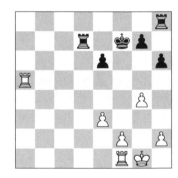

critical was: 27...h5 28.gxh5 ♖d5 29.♖xd5 exd5, and Black's pawns are split, but the white h-pawn is weak, too, and I think Black should hold. **27...♖c8 28.♖b1 ♖c2 29.♖a8 ♖c4 30.h3**

30...h5? Definitely a bad moment, since the tactics now work for White. **31.gxh5 ♖h4 32.♖h8**

32...♔f6 The first point is that if 32...♖xh3, then 33.♔g2 ♖h4 34.f4 traps the rook.
33.♔h2! Leaving the g-file open.
33...♖d5 34.♖f8+

34...♔e7
34...♔g5 would lose instantly to 35.♖g1+ and 36.♖h8 mate.

Vladimir Kramnik and Anish Giri at their last press conference after the Dutchman had defended himself with great accuracy to save the draw.

35.♖f3 ♖f5 36.♖xf5 exf5 37.♖g1 ♔f6 38.♖g6+ ♔f7 39.♖g5 ♔f6 40.f4 And Adams resigned.

Caruana simply, if I may say so, played too much chess in the second half of 2014. His form in St. Louis in September was so out of this world that there was bound to be a reaction. This continued in London, where he was a little flat. After his first-round loss and three draws, he got into trouble against Nakamura in the final round, but rallied and came close to winning.

You can see the final scores in the cross-table. Under the football method Adams was ahead of Caruana by virtue of having won a game, even though he was behind under normal currency. The main idea of 3, 1, 0 is, as I understand it, to promote more aggressive chess, and perhaps more risk taking. With such great players this seems unnecessary – they'll fight whenever they can, but will not take unreasonable risks – and personally I'm not greatly pro it. But what the scoring system does do is to allow big swings in a single round, and everybody apart from Caruana had a chance to take first before the final round, which was certainly exciting. ■

London 2014				1	2	3	4	5	6		TPR
1 **Vishy Anand**	IGM	IND	2793	*	1	1	1	3	1	7	2849
2 **Vladimir Kramnik**	IGM	RUS	2769	1	*	1	3	1	1	7	2854
3 **Anish Giri**	IGM	NED	2768	1	1	*	1	3	1	7	2854
4 **Hikaru Nakamura**	IGM	USA	2775	1	0	1	*	3	1	6	2781
5 **Michael Adams**	IGM	ENG	2745	0	1	0	0	*	3	4	2638
6 **Fabiano Caruana**	IGM	ITA	2829	1	1	1	1	0	*	4	2698
3 points for a win, 1 for a draw											

Fair & Square

Vishy Anand: 'There are some things we do much better than computers, but since most of chess is tactical based they do many things better than humans. And this imbalance remains. I no longer have any issues. It's a bit like asking an astronomer, does he mind that a telescope does all the work? He is used to it. It is just an incredible tool that you can use.'

Oleg Romanishin: 'If one would cancel all traffic rules and switch off all traffic lights, watching city traffic on TV would be also awfully interesting!'
(The Ukrainian GM on FIDE's efforts to make chess a TV spectator sport)

Hans Ree: 'When you have a world champion in your smartphone, the myth of the superior brainpower of human chess champions has lost its power.'

David Bronstein: 'The most powerful weapon in chess is to have the next move.'

Amir Khan: 'It's going to be like a game of chess – hit and move. It's whoever comes out stronger.'
(The British boxer before his successful Las Vegas WBC Welterweight title defence bout against Devon Alexander)

Andy Carroll: 'He knows how to beat managers and their tactics. He knows what they are going to do against us. It's just a game of chess, really, looking a move ahead.'
(The West Ham United striker, speaking about his manager, Sam Allardyce)

John van der Wiel:'When you absolutely don't know what to do anymore, it is time to panic.'

Wilhelm Steinitz: 'Chess is so inspiring that I do not believe a good player is capable of having an evil thought during the game.'

George Bernard Shaw: '[Chess is] a foolish expedient for making idle people believe they are doing something very clever, when they are only wasting their time.'

Ryan Giggs: 'Xavi is a bit like a chess player. He is always two or three steps ahead of everybody else. For me, he is one of the greatest players ever who played for one of the best teams ever.'
(The Manchester United assistant manager, in praise of Barcelona midfielder Xavi Hernandez, who has now equalled his 151 Champions' League appearances)

David Norwood: 'What we need are lots of girls who aren't as good as us, who'll treat us with the proper respect and reverence.'

Barack Obama: 'There was a spate of stories about how he is the chess master and outmanoeuvring the West and outmanoeuvring Mr. Obama and this and that and the other. And right now, he's presiding over the collapse of his currency, a major financial crisis and a huge economic contraction.'
(The American President on Russian President Vladimir Putin, during a pre-Christmas interview with CNN)

H.G Wells: 'You have, let us say, a promising politician, a rising artist that you wish to destroy. Dagger or bomb are archaic, clumsy, and unreliable – but teach him, inoculate him with chess! Our statesmen would sit with pocket boards while the country went to the devil, and our breadwinners would forget their wives in seeking after impossible mates.'
(In Concerning Chess, 1901)

Reuben Fine: 'Combinations have always been the most intriguing aspect of Chess. The masters look for them, the public applauds them, the critics praise them. It is because combinations are possible that Chess is more than a lifeless mathematical exercise. They are the poetry of the game; they are to Chess what melody is to music. They represent the triumph of mind over matter.'

Sir Clive Woodward: 'The skills used in chess are transferable to all types of sport because it makes you think... It's how you develop those thinking and understanding skills – especially in football and rugby when often you are playing phases ahead, the ball may be going one way but you are thinking further forward and that's what chess is all about.'
(The former England Rugby World Cup-winning manager, speaking to The Rugby Player magazine at the ProBiz Cup at the London Chess Classic)

Tobias Wolff: 'One can imagine a world without essays. It would be a little poorer, of course, like a world without chess, but one could live in it.'

MAXIMize your Tactics

with Maxim Notkin

Find the best move in the positions below

Solutions on page 105

1. White to play

2. White to play

3. Black to play

4. White to play

5. Black to play

6. Black to play

7. White to play

8. White to play

9. Black to play

'Chess teaches you to lose'

Miguel Najdorf's life of tragedy and triumph

Of few people could it be genuinely said that chess saved their life. Miguel Najdorf is one such man. If he had not been playing at the 1939 Chess Olympiad in Buenos Aires, when the Second World War broke out back in Europe, he would almost certainly have perished in the Nazi death camps in Poland, along with the rest of his family. From these tragic beginnings, this remarkable man went on to live a life that could have come straight out of a novel. Indeed, some have claimed that he was the model for the character of Mirko Czentovic in Stefan Zweig's **Schachnovelle.** Najdorf created his own mythologies and it is often very difficult to disentangle the fact from the legend.

Adam Feinstein

Miguel Najdorf:
'Chess teaches us the spirit of solidarity.
It teaches us not to hate one another.'

W

We do know that he was born Mojsze Mendel (Mieczyslaw) Najdorf, the eldest of five children, into a Jewish family in Grodzisk Mazowiecki, near Warsaw, on April 15, 1910. His parents were Gdalik and Raisa. A sister, Ines, died in a skiing accident at the age of 12. Najdorf's daughter Liliana – whose 2008 book, *Najdorf x Najdorf*, relies almost entirely on the accounts he gave her – claims that he was 14 years old when he was first taught chess by a friend's father, a violinist with the Warsaw Philhamonic. Najdorf was hooked immediately. His mother, Raisa, strongly disapproved of his new passion, however – so strongly, in fact, that she threw his chess set into the fireplace. But Najdorf was spurred on by the maternal opposition, although he did begin studying to become a mathematics teacher at the Warsaw Polytechnic – a course he did not complete.

He claimed as his main and greatest teacher, Savielly Tartakower, an extraordinary man in his own right. Born in Russia, he became first a Polish citizen before taking on French nationality. He could write poetry in three languages. 'I learned to play at his side. He was a humanist, a fine humorist, a man of great culture, an extraordinary being, a great man from every point of view,' Najdorf would say of Tartakower in later years.

Najdorf played his first National Tournament in Poland in 1928 at the age of 18. He took fifth place but won all three 'brilliancy prizes' – an early recognition of his flair for attacking combinations. By 1930, he was recognized as one of the strongest players in Warsaw. At around this time, he was called up to military service in the border region between Poland and Germany. He reached the rank of sub-lieutenant but, if his own claims are to be believed, he narrowly escaped being shot for accidentally deserting one Sunday.

Najdorf became champion of Warsaw in 1934 and, the following year, finished equal second in the Polish championship in Warsaw behind Tartakower. Julian Mafdes, writing in the Lvov daily *Chwili* (The Waves), said: 'A talent has emerged such as we have not seen for ages.' Other journalists suggested Najdorf needed to put on weight and control his nerves. After the Warsaw tournament, Najdorf played a training match with Tartakower at the Italia chess café in Torun. Najdorf, apparently wearing his Polish Army uniform, pulled off a huge surprise, defeating his mentor.

This performance prompted Tartakower and the Polish Chess Federation to appeal to the country's Armed Forces Ministry to grant Najdorf a period of leave to play for Poland in the 6th Chess Olympiad which took place a few months later in Warsaw. The Polish team came third, behind the United States and Sweden. Najdorf, playing mainly on board three, won nine games, drew six and lost only two. In that tournament, according to some sources, he beat Glucksberg in a famous sacrificial game later dubbed 'the Polish Immortal'. Other sources give the date as 1929. However, the highly respected Polish chess historian, Tomasz Lissowski, tells me that the celebrated game was probably played in 1930, in the local tournament in Warsaw. It was certainly published in a chess column in a Warsaw newspaper in 1930 and so, according to Lissowski, it could not possibly have been played as late as the 1935 Olympiad.

The newspaper, *Nasz Przeglad* (Our

View), left us with this entertaining description at the time of the 25-year-old, still known as Mieczyslaw Najdorf: 'Nature has not over-endowed him with good looks but chess players are predicting immense success for him. He is a character apart, unbalanced, amusing. All of a sudden, he will stand up from the chessboard and yawn. He is extremely emotional. It is hard to imagine that this game played with wooden pieces, accessible even to grey-haired old men, can bring him contentment. Najdorf cannot sit still. During his opponent's thinking time, he will stroll around between the tables and peer at the other games, then he will have to wander across the hall looking for his own table when it is his turn to move.'

In 1936, Najdorf both completed his military service and married for the first time. His wife, Genia, a talented pianist, had scandalously called off her engagement to another man to marry him. Najdorf still found time to give two simultaneous displays during their honeymoon, in Zakopane and Krakow.

In some ways, one of the most remarkable tournaments of Najdorf's entire

Miguel Najdorf with his first wife Genia, a talented pianist, who would be killed in the Holocaust with the rest of his family.

'He is a character apart, unbalanced, amusing. All of a sudden, he will stand up from the chessboard and yawn.'

chess career took place in Munich in August-September, 1936. This 'Schach-Olympia' was an unofficial 'Olympiad', organized by the German Chess Federation as a counterpart to the Olympic Games in Berlin that same year. Initially, Najdorf flatly refused to play in an event held in a nation ruled by the Nazis and was persuaded to do so only after lengthy discussions with the president of the Polish Chess Federation, Bronislaw Pilsudski.

Genia was outraged at what she saw as her new husband's act of 'betrayal' but, as he recalled later, 'I went up in her esteem when Poland came second (to Hungary) and I won the gold medal.' In an extraordinary, and sinister, turn of events, Najdorf received his medal in Munich from a certain Hans Frank who, just a few years later, as governor-general of Nazi-occupied Poland, would be responsible for overseeing the extermination of Najdorf's entire family in the Holocaust.

At the Margate tournament in 1939, Najdorf was invited to substitute a player who had dropped out of the tournament. For the first time, Najdorf would be testing himself in a tournament against many of the world's strongest players, including the Cuban former World Champion. José Raúl Capablanca; the Estonian Paul Keres and the Czech Salo Flohr. As it happened, Margate proved a disappointment – he finished down in sixth place – although he did draw his game against Capablanca with the black pieces. He told Liliana many years later that, while he arrived at the board exhausted after a sleepless night of preparation, Capablanca turned up for their game in the company of two women and, after playing each move, would casually retire to enjoy their adulation. But after Najdorf produced a double-edged continuation, Capa, apparently caught by surprise, offered a draw. Najdorf shocked the onlookers by declining, despite the fact that he had just a minute left on the clock to play 18 moves.

In August 1939, Najdorf set sail for the Buenos Aires Olympiad, the first ever Olympiad on Latin American soil. It was just a month before the Nazis invaded Poland. In a fateful decision, Genia, who was suffering from the flu, decided to remain behind in Warsaw with their young daughter, Lusha.

Najdorf, although the captain of the Polish team in Buenos Aires, ceded top board to Tartakower. Poland took the silver medal, just half a point behind the victors, Germany. Najdorf once again won the gold medal. But he could not celebrate. On September 1, the Polish Ambassador in Buenos Aires, Zdzislaw Kurnikowski, announced the Nazi invasion of Poland during Najdorf's game with the Dutchman, Nico Cortlever. Although Najdorf held the advantage in this game, the news from Poland was so distressing that he went on to lose it.

In desperation, he tried to bring his family out of Poland, appealing to Argentina's President Roberto María Ortiz and to Kurnikowski. Neither could help. Najdorf's father, Gdalik, died in the Warsaw Ghetto in 1943, and the remaining members of the family were sent either to Auschwitz or Treblinka death camps. They included his wife, Genia, and their daughter Lusha.

It is difficult to imagine the emotional toll such a tragedy took on Najdorf. He recalled later: 'There were 300 people in my family and not one of them survived.' Perhaps this was not quite true. He was once travelling in the New York subway when he noticed a man reading a Polish newspaper. They started talking and the man revealed himself to be a cousin of Najdorf's. Intriguingly,

during a visit Najdorf made to Israel in 1996 – just a year before his death – the Israeli chess magazine *Shahmat* published an interview with him together with Esther Salzman, whom the magazine described as 'his cousin, the last scion of his Polish family.'

'I remained in Buenos Aires without speaking the language,' Najdorf said, 'all alone and with two hundred dollars in my pocket. I thought I was going crazy, but chess helped me. Chess teaches you to lose.' According to Liliana, Najdorf was faced with the decision of whether to stay on in Buenos Aires or leave for Cuba, where an uncle was living (after fleeing Poland for refusing to serve in the Army). Capablanca, it seems, attempted to lure Najdorf to Havana, but he was starting to enjoy life in the Buenos Aires boarding house he shared with Paul Keres in the Calle Lavalle.

Having decided to remain in Argentina, Najdorf changed his name in mid-1940 from Mendel (or Mieczyslaw) to Miguel Najdorf and began earning a living by selling ties and perfume in the Jewish quarter of Buenos Aires, the Once. For a while, he also taught chess in the Newell's Old Boys Club in the city of Rosario, about 170 miles northwest of Buenos Aires.

Another way he began to make money was to take advantage of his prodigious memory. First, he was a 'mnemotechnician' – he appeared in shows where he memorized numbers on a piece of paper. He said these shows proved very lucrative but were 'crippling'. Then he began giving simultaneous chess displays around Argentina. Here, his chief motive seems to have been a desire to alert any possible surviving relatives back home in Poland as to his whereabouts. His chess-playing exploits did indeed reach his homeland – but no family members were alive to receive the news.

His feats were certainly noteworthy. In 1940, just a year after settling in Buenos Aires, he set the world record for a blindfold simultaneous display in Rosario. Of the 40 games, he won

'On a plane or a train, I read chess books as if they were detective novels.'

36, drew three and lost just one. This record could not be ratified, however, because it was not witnessed by international observers. No matter. In October 1943, he became 'World Blindfold Champion', again in Rosario, and then went on to beat his own record in a rainstorm in Sao Paulo on January 25, 1947. In fact, on this occasion in Brazil, although there were 45 boards, the games took so long that he graciously allowed his exhausted opponents to be substituted, so he actually played against a total of 83 opponents. He himself changed his suit once because of the storm. Asked later whether it was true that he could not sleep for days afterwards and that he had finally dozed off in a cinema, Najdorf replied: 'Yes, it is. Can you imagine how bad that movie must have been?' His Sao Paolo blindfold record was finally superseded by George Koltanowski in San Francisco in 1961.

In around 1941, a friend – some sources claim that it was the Argentinian chess player Carlos Guimard – suggested that Najdorf take up work as an insurance salesman. According to his future son-in-law, Víctor Solnicki, Najdorf first worked for Sun Life of Canada and National Western Life, before later joining Jackson National Life, for whom he acted as their general agent outside the United States. 'Miguel was a very talented person and he made a lot of money selling insurance policies to very rich people in Argentina, Brazil, Chile, Uruguay, Paraguay and Venezuela.' Solnicki told Tomasz Lissowski.

The Argentinian chess writer and correspondence chess grandmaster, Juan Sebastián Morgado, told me in Buenos Aires that Najdorf had even travelled to Paraguay to draw up a highly lucrative insurance policy for the dictator, General Alfredo Stroessner. This was confirmed to Morgado by the Chilean International Master, René Letelier.

In 1944, Najdorf officially became an Argentinian citizen. He would often say that the finest move he ever played was deciding to stay on and live in Buenos Aires.

Between 1939 and 1946, Najdorf won – or was placed equal first in – fifteen tournaments. In August and September 1946, Groningen in the Netherlands staged the first major international tournament after the end of the Second World War. The event also marked the first time that the Soviet Union ever sent a team to an event outside the USSR. His old friend and mentor, Tartakower, was now representing France and the US participants included Samuel Reshevsky and Reuben Fine. The Soviet contingent was led by Mikhail Botvinnik, who was leading the tournament with one round to go. In that final round, Najdorf defeated Botvinnik and won 500 Dutch guilders through a bet with another, unknown player or journalist – Najdorf would prove to be a life-long gambler, like his own father.

The 37-year-old Najdorf was not short on confidence. In 1947, he wrote

> ## 'If they invite me to the next tournament for the World Championships, I will definitely win.'

six articles for the Argentinian publication, *Mundo Argentino*, entitled 'I will be World Champion.' Here, he declared: 'I have come to the conclusion that, if they invite me to the next tournament for the World Championships, I will definitely win. I concede that my future opponents have the upper hand in the openings. But I play my own lines and have my very own openings. I'm studying and there will be some surprises in store. I have novelties which I am keeping for the right moment. As for the middle game, I don't think anyone is better than me. My play has undergone a natural and beneficial evolution. In my youth, I loved wonderful, brilliant combinations. But later on, I came to understand the beauty of Capablanca's play: it was simple yet more difficult and beautiful than the spectacular sacrifice. As for the endgame, that's one of my strong points. But my real strength lies in gaining the initiative. I believe the hardest thing in chess is to win a won game. My strength is in being able to finish off a game accurately and at times I have achieved Capablanca's machine-like precision.'

He added: 'If the World Champion has to be a complete man, capable of dominating all styles of play, then I can become World Champion. Maybe I'm being a little excessive, but I don't find too many difficulties playing chess. It does not wear me out, because my strength does not always lie in calculation but in intuition. On a plane or a train, I read chess books as if they were detective novels.'

As it turned out, Najdorf never did get a chance to play a match for the world title. According to some sources, Mikhail Botvinnik did not like Najdorf's fun-loving nature – in particular the open joy he had demonstrated after defeating him at Groningen – and played a leading role in blocking Najdorf's access to the world title cycle. Héctor Rossetto – the Argentinian grandmaster and director of the 1978 Buenos Aires Olympiad – told Juan Sebastián Morgado that, when Botvinnik heard how Najdorf had made a bet that he would beat him in Groningen, Botvinnik began cursing the man he called 'the capitalist pig' and instructed the Soviet delegation that they must do all in their power to prevent Najdorf playing for the world title. According to Morgado, Botvinnik managed to have the list of Candidates for the 1948 World Championship eliminator tournament (divided between The Hague and Moscow) reduced from eight to just six, and even when Reuben Fine dropped out, Najdorf was not allowed to take his place. Botvinnik himself won the tournament convincingly.

Morgado is convinced that Botvinnik wielded sufficient power at this point to ensure that Najdorf was not invited to compete for the world title. 'The Soviet political system allowed Botvinnik enormous advantages. And FIDE itself was controlled by the USSR Chess Federation. The Botvinnik-Keres match in the same tournament, in which Botvinnik won the first four games, was completely anomalous.'

However, Tomasz Lissowski disagrees. He told me: 'In 1948, Botvinnik was – in my opinion – not in a position to dictate his wishes to the whole chess world. That would be a major exaggeration. The six players – Euwe, Fine, Reshevsky, Smyslov, Keres and Botvinnik – apparently did not want to share the honours with anyone else. None of those six voted for Najdorf, who, as the winner of the tournament in Prague, did have some right to be there. But in any case, they were stronger than Najdorf in 1948.'

In April 1947, Najdorf met the woman who would become his second wife. Adela Jusid – known to all as Eta – was a shy young Jewish woman who loved reading and swimming. Their first encounter took place at the home of Cecilio Skliar (the Argentinian Chess Federation's chief physician) and his wife Dorita. Just two weeks later, on May 19, they were married. Whenever Liliana asked him many years afterwards: 'Why the rush?' he would reply: 'I'm a gambler. I wanted to start a family and I knew she was just the girl I needed: Jewish, with impeccable parents, she had noble sentiments and she was a good-looking girl. What more could I hope for?'

According to Liliana, however, Eta was not so sure she had made the right choice. Najdorf was often travelling and reports reached her of his occasional dalliances with other women. They had two daughters: Mirta, born in February 1948, and Liliana herself in March 1952. Najdorf set eyes on Liliana for the first time only four months after her birth, because he was in Cuba at the time. Liliana always reproached her father for being absent at this and other important occasions: 'I scarcely remember him at any of my birthdays, never when I was ill, or at New Year, at school meetings or in any of the situations when a child really needs a father to be there.'

At the same time, Najdorf could be 'dictatorial' when he was at home, 'and I hated him for that,' Liliana wrote in her book. She told me in Buenos Aires that her father was 'both absent and omnipresent'. Their relationship was clearly a complex one. She conceded that her father always returned from his trips abroad laden with presents: 'He was electric, different, captivating, bewildering and exhausting – marvellous.'

Meanwhile, Najdorf himself cut a dash as a man about town. He was a *bon vivant* and was always immaculately turned out. 'El Viejo' (The Old Man), as he came affectionately to be known long before he *was* old, also

MAX EUWE CENTRE AMSTERDAM

Analysing with former World Champion Max Euwe at the 1950 Olympiad in Dubrovnik. In the middle Herman Steiner (moustache) and Samuel Reshevsky look on.

seems to have been a keen pursuer of the opposite sex. According to Liliana, he had a girlfriend, Carmen, while living for a while in Rosario, but when he fell for one of Carmen's closest (married) friends, the husband found out and promised to hunt him down with a shotgun. Najdorf quickly fled Rosario, leaving all his possessions behind.

As his son-in-law, Victor Solnicki, married to Mirta, put it to Tomasz Lissowski: 'He liked all sorts of things: travelling first class, eating first class, wearing first-class clothes, reading books, classical music, movies, soccer, everything. He enjoyed every minute of his life like no one else in this world. Miguel played cards for money at the strongest tables in the cities, and believe me he was a winner. He applied the chess player's way of thinking to the business of life. First the idea, then the move, in life, as in chess; and when you lose a game, you must think about the next one, because if you keep thinking about the one you have lost, you are sure to lose the next one, too.'

Najdorf played in the first-ever Interzonal tournament, in June 1948, in the Swedish health resort of Saltsjöbaden.

The top five players, according to the new rules, would earn the right to play in the Candidates' Tournament for the world title, but Najdorf finished only joint sixth after blundering in a won pawn endgame against Alexander Kotov.

The end of the 1940s saw the birth of the so-called Najdorf Variation of the Sicilian Defence – which would later become a firm favourite of both Bobby Fischer and Garry Kasparov – and in 1950, Najdorf was named one of the 27 first official FIDE grandmasters. In April 1950, he was admitted to the Candidates' Tournament in Budapest. He finished in fifth place with nine points, which was insufficient to allow him access to the next stage of the World Championship cycle. By general consensus, this was the closest Najdorf ever came to the world crown. He tried again at the 1953 Candidates' Tournament in Zurich, where he won the brilliancy prize but came only joint sixth.

At a match in 1954 between Argentina and the Soviet Union, organized by the government of President Juan Perón at the Teatro Cervantes in Buenos Aires, Najdorf found himself pitted against the Soviet champion, David Bronstein. Perón made the symbolic first move: 1.e4. But after the President left, Najdorf took back the move and played 1.d4 instead. An astounded Bronstein could not believe anyone would dare to go against the President's wishes in this way. 'I reassured him that we were living in a democracy,' Najdorf wrote later.

In fact, a military coup toppled the Perón government the very next year. According to Najdorf's fellow Argentinian grandmaster, Oscar Panno, the new regime refused to fund the Argentinian team's travel to the 12th Olympiad in Moscow in 1956. In the end, Najdorf somehow persuaded officials at the Soviet Embassy in Vienna to ensure their onward passage. However, for the first time since the Second World War, Argentina failed to take a medal at an Olympiad, finishing in fourth place.

That was a major blow for Najdorf, who not long before had suffered a crushing personal disappointment, only able to occupy a lowly twelfth position at the Interzonal in Gothenburg in 1955. According to Salo Flohr, Najdorf 'normally a cheerful, self-confident person. went to pieces for much of the time. His loud voice, with its constant laughter and jokes, was no longer to be heard.'

The dispiriting results continued. In 1957, Najdorf failed to qualify for the Zonal tournament in Rio de Janeiro. Oscar Panno says this hurt him deeply and he abandoned the FIDE cycle from then on, no longer playing for the world title, either in zonals or interzonals.

Not that Najdorf gave up competitive chess. Far from it. With typical optimism and energy, he once again began to notch up remarkable tournament victories. He took joint first place with the Czech Ludek Pachman at the Mar del Plata tournament in 1959, ahead of a 16-year-old Bobby Fischer.

At the end of the 1950s, Najdorf moved temporarily to Venezuela. The *British Chess Magazine* claimed in 1960 that he became involved in importing

porcelain from Japan, but there is no evidence whatsoever to support this. Other sources maintain that he wanted to make a permanent move to Venezuela to benefit from the oil boom but that Eta preferred to live in Buenos Aires to bring up Mirta and Liliana. Meanwhile, Najdorf continued to travel the globe. In November 1960, he paid an emotional visit to Poland and received a rapturous welcome when he gave simultaneous displays in Warsaw and Lodz.

At the 1962 Olympiad in Varna, Bulgaria – where Najdorf again won the Gold Medal – Boris Spassky recalled witnessing a game in which Najdorf was short of time. 'He had only about one minute left for ten moves and at precisely that moment, a pretty young girl came up to him and asked him to smile for a photograph. Najdorf turned his head to face her, smiled – and still had time to win the game.'

That same year, Najdorf took first prize at the first Capablanca Memorial Tournament in Havana, winning nine games in a row. Both Fidel Castro and Che Guevara were said to have watched some of the games. Typically, Najdorf spent the prize money (it was awarded in non-convertible Cuban pesos) on inviting his friends to a three-day binge at the Tropicana night club in Havana. He also maintained that Che invited him to give a blindfold simultaneous display against the members of the government. Fidel was apparently on first board, his brother Raúl on second and the Cuban President, Osvaldo Dorticós, on third, with Che himself down on eighth board. He recalled that he drew with Fidel and offered Che a draw, which was declined. Che said he wanted his revenge for a previous

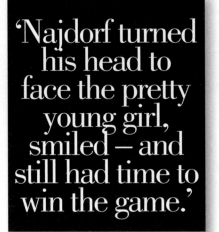

'Najdorf turned his head to face the pretty young girl, smiled – and still had time to win the game.'

defeat Najdorf had handed out to him at a simultaneous in Mar del Plata in 1947. The game continued and Najdorf went on to win again.

Najdorf claimed to have played against a number of other major political personalities, including the Shah of Iran, Yugoslavia's Marshal Tito and Britain's wartime Prime Minister, Winston Churchill. And not just politicians. He apparently played two games with the violinist Yehudi Menuhin at the Hotel Plaza in Buenos Aires in 1975. That must have appealed to Najdorf's passion for music. After all he had learnt to play chess from a violinist, married a pianist and two of his five grandchildren became musicians.

According to Liliana, Najdorf was 'apolitical'. However, Juan Sebastián Morgado claims that he spent a great deal of time with Juan Perón and even received a new car from the President as a gift. Indeed, as Morgado points out, Najdorf's own book, *15 Aspirantes al Título Mundial* (15 Challengers for the World Title), contains a photograph in which he is sporting the coat of arms of the Peronist Party. There are also suggestions in some quarters that Najdorf enjoyed good relations with Argentina's military dictatorship of Jorge Videla in the 1970s and 1980s. Liliana herself notes in her book that her father received full military honours at his funeral.

In 1971, one of Argentina's leading dailies, *Clarín*, invited him to write a regular weekly chess column every Saturday. This contract coincided with a peak in popularity for chess in Argentina: with the Candidates' Final match taking place in Buenos Aires between Fischer and Tigran Petrosian at the time, most shops in the capital had completely sold out of chess sets.

Najdorf continued to travel the world

tirelessly. He was in Reykjavik in 1972 to cover the Fischer-Spassky world title match for *Clarín*. That same year, he also toured the Far East, giving simultaneous displays in India, Iran, Thailand, Indonesia and Japan. During the Haifa Olympiad in 1976, a rich businessman whose wife had just died offered him 3,000 dollars to stay on for a week to play chess to ease his boredom. Najdorf accepted.

Najdorf's own wife, Eta, died on August 21, 1977. Three years later, he married for the third and final time. He had actually met Rita Dvoskin not long after he arrived in Argentina. At the time, she was married to a Socialist lawyer (and chess lover), Jacobo Caplansky. In the late-1940s, Rita and Jacobo had published a magazine together in opposition to the Perón regime. Under the second Perón administration, the couple were forced to leave their home town of General Pico, in the central province of La Pampa, and move to Buenos Aires. After Jacobo died there suddenly one day while playing chess, Najdorf and Rita grew close and they married in 1980.

Rita proved a very loving wife to Miguel. Liliana describes her combing and dressing him 'as if he were a baby, accompanying him to the chess club until the early hours of the morning.' And he returned her affection. With great honesty, Liliana says that she felt pangs of jealousy when she saw her father and Rita embracing and singing together for years afterwards, 'like a pair of newly-weds'. In similar vein, perhaps, Liliana also told me that she hated chess because it was a rival for her father's affections.

Najdorf kept up his routine of between five and 20 games of rapid chess per day. The American grandmaster, Larry Evans, recalled: 'Najdorf improved at an age when most masters decline, and it was a joy to be in his company. Even at 68, he never tired of playing speed games with me all night in Sao Paulo; one morning I barely escaped with a draw against him in the tournament.' Juan Sebastián Mor-

Celebrating his 80th birthday with his daughters Mirta and Liliana, the author of *Najdorf x Najdorf*.

gado told me: 'Psychologically, Najdorf could not look back. Remembering was torture for him. So he decided on action, action and more action, playing blitz chess. It was his drug, right up until the end of his life.'

In 1978, the 23rd Olympiad returned to Buenos Aires after 39 years – and six months after Argentina won the football World Cup on home soil. Unfortunately, not a single participant from 1939 took part this time around. Najdorf and the other strongest Argentinian players (including Panno and Quinteros) were not available, having missed the Argentinian Championship, which was the only qualifying tournament. But the following year, Najdorf shared second place (with Boris Spassky among others) at the Buenos Aires International Tournament.

One of his last great tournaments was perhaps also one of his most bizarre: in Bugojno, in former Yugoslavia, in 1982. He was actually the director of the event but when Mikhail Tal dropped out through illness, leaving the number of players at what was considered to be an unlucky 13, the city's mayor begged Najdorf to play. He agreed, but only reluctantly because he was ill-prepared. Although he fin-

ished in equal eleventh place, he missed a draw against the eventual winner of the tournament, the 19-year-old Gary Kasparov.

By now, Najdorf was one of the world's oldest active grandmasters. In 1984, while playing at the Mar del Plata tournament, *Clarín* sent him a touching seventy-fourth birthday present: a cake decorated with a chess board set up in the Najdorf Variation.

In 1988, Najdorf was appointed Advisor for Sports in the Argentinian Senate. The following year, he shared fourth place at the Argentinian Championship. Two years later, on April 15, 1990, the inaugural Miguel Najdorf Tournament opened at the Teatro San Martín in Buenos Aires to mark his eightieth birthday. It has since become one of the most important tournaments in Latin America's chess calendar.

His last national championship was in 1991. But three years later, in 1994, he took part in the International Open in Mar del Plata and finished unbeaten, an extraordinary achievement for a man of 84. And that was not the end of the story: in what was to prove his final competitive appearance, he took six

Komodo Chess 8 – the new No. 1!

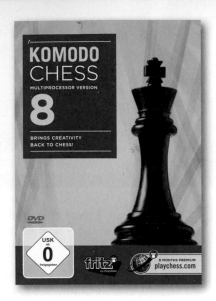

Komodo is a chess program that is different from the rest. Its search makes greater use of extensions than any other top engine, which results in a slightly lower average depth, helps the actual playing strength significantly. It also allows Komodo to often see deeper than any other engine, even if it is displaying a lower search depth. The evaluation differs from its main rivals because unlike the automated tuning generally employed the Komodo evaluation represents a blend of both automated tuning and the judgment of a grandmaster and computer expert (Larry Kaufman). The programming team have avoided terms and weights that don't make sense to him, even if they happen to test a bit positively. Automated evaluations are subject to rather large sample error, and applying some chess judgment appears to be beneficial, both in results and in the reasonableness of reported evaluations.

Komodo is primarily known for superb positional play. Of course it also one of the top few engines in tactical strength, but the programmers have not been willing to sacrifice positional play just to score better on tactical problem sets. It is generally recognized that all good engines are far stronger tactically than any human player, but that when positional judgment is involved, top grandmasters are still superior in many positions to any engine. Therefore I think it makes sense to emphasize positional play rather than tactical skill; it is better to improve one's weakest point rather than just to further improve the strongest feature.

Komodo is especially useful for opening analysis, because as an opening specialist Larry Kaufman has always paid close attention to checking whether the program's evaluations in the opening agree in general with accepted theory. Another point in which Komodo excels is the play and evaluation of positions with material imbalance, which it handles more correctly than other top engines. The endgame of Komodo has been improved by the use of Syzygy tablebases, which are considered the best for actual play and game analysis as they provide only the most essential information to save time and memory.

Another unique feature in Komodo is its superior handling of multiple processors. This is most noticeable when using eight or more cores. There is little doubt that Komodo 8 is and will remain the top rated commercial chess engine on most rating lists.

What you get:
- Komodo 8 chess engine (64 bit)
- the new Deep Fritz 64-bit program interface (+32 bit program interface)
- Premium membership to playchess (6 months)

79,90 €

Parimarjan Negi: The Modern Scotch Opening

The Scotch has long been associated with exciting play, although people often doubt it's positional base. But the opening has evolved from the swashbuckling games of the 19th century to become a sound, but aggressive, alternative to the evergreen Spanish. In his first Fritz-Trainer DVD, Parimarjan Negi looks at the latest revolution in Scotch theory that has completely changed white's plans, and once again brought back the interest of the world's elite. Negi presents not only the white strategies in detail but also outlines a dynamic way for Black to counter this latest trend.

Parimarjan Negi (21) became the youngest GM in the world in 2006, and since then has won many international events, including the Asian Championship in 2012. At the chess olympiad in Tromso he won bronze with India, with a 2730 Elo performance on board one.

29,90 €

CHESSBASE GMBH · OSTERBEKSTRASSE 90A · D-22083 HAMBURG · TEL ++(49) 40/639060-12 · FAX ++(49) 40/6301282 · WWW.CHESSBASE.COM · INFO@CHESSBASE.COM
CHESSBASE DEALER: NEW IN CHESS · P.O. Box 1093 · NL-1810 KB Alkmaar · phone (+31)72 5127137 · fax (+31)72 5158234 · WWW.NEWINCHESS.COM

and a half points from nine games at Mar del Plata in 1996, just a year before his death.

Right up to the end, he still indulged his passion for lightning chess and still came out with glorious witticisms ('I won't play with you any more – you have insulted my friend,' he told one blitz opponent who had cursed himself for a blunder). He also continued to go into his insurance office in Buenos Aires. His company now employed more than 100 people.

He won the Argentinian championship eight times – more often than anyone else. In all, he won a total of 52 international tournaments. During the course of more than six decades, he had played against 11 of the 19 World Champions, beating Botvinnik, Smyslov, Petrosian, Tal and Fischer.

Although Capablanca and Fischer were his favourite players, he also expressed immense admiration for Garry Kasparov. He compared Kasparov's passion with that of the violinist, Itzhak Perlman. Kasparov repaid the compliment: 'If only half the young players of today felt half the love Miguel Najdorf feels for chess.'

Chess was also where he felt at his calmest, where his impatience could not get the better of him. And he could be very impatient. When his car broke down while he was in India, he was told he would have to wait a week for it to be mended. The only alternative was an elephant: 'I'm no good at waiting. I chose the elephant immediately. We spent four days on top of that animal which kept tottering from side to side. I couldn't sit down for a whole month afterwards, but it was still preferable to waiting around doing nothing.'

Najdorf saw chess as good for forging character. He considered it fundamental to teach the game in schools. And, more than anything, he said, chess 'teaches us the spirit of solidarity. It teaches us not to hate one another.' Nevertheless, he could bear grudges. In fact, Liliana told me he 'fought with everyone'. After his friend and fellow

Argentinian, Jorge Szmetan, turned down a draw offer against him at a tournament and went on to win the game, Najdorf refused to speak to him for a long time afterwards.

Miguel Angel Quinteros, the Argentinian chess grandmaster, told me in Buenos Aires: 'Every time we played each other, it turned into a battle. We had terrible quarrels.' Things came to a head during a game in a Saturday rapid five-minute tournament at the Alfil Negro (Black Bishop) Club in Buenos Aires. Najdorf was very short of time and began to move the pieces with one hand and press his clock with the other – which is completely illegal. When Quinteros persistently told him to stop, Najdorf eventually picked up the pieces, threw them at him and began to insult him in the most grotesque terms. Quinteros successfully sued for slander but when Najdorf was sentenced to 18 months' imprisonment, Quinteros agreed to drop all charges if Najdorf would organize six rapid chess tournaments a year in Argentina and put up the prize money. Najdorf accepted the offer immediately. Although the relationship between the two men was strained from then on, Quinteros wept openly when Najdorf died. 'I deeply regretted having transferred our chess board battles into our lives,' Quinteros told me in Buenos Aires. 'We had a very strong friendship, despite our differences.'

Rita's deterioration into Alzheimer's and her death on June 2, 1996 hit Najdorf very hard. He had married three times and been widowed each time. Liliana once asked her father whether he himself was afraid of death. He shook his head and replied: 'No. When the time comes, I hope it's mate in one. The only thing I fear is pain and remaining an invalid.'

Shortly before he died, Liliana had written him a letter in which she declared: 'It's not easy being the daughter of a monster. They can sometimes be insatiable and no food is enough for them. [But] in general, monsters give out a great deal, as well, and you have to be ready to receive it. They devour

instead of eating, they lecture instead of talking and lay down the rules instead of expressing opinions. They adore instead of loving. It is not easy or comfortable having a monster for a father; he makes a lot of noise and casts a large shadow. And yet, despite the problems, it is still a privilege.'

Miguel Najdorf died in Málaga, in the south of Spain, on July 4, 1997 from complications following heart surgery. He was 87. He had travelled to Europe despite his doctors' advice (he is reported to have said: 'Get me on the plane – I want to die watching a chess tournament') and, true to form, he was gambling in a casino when he began to feel ill.

The tributes quickly flooded in. Anatoly Karpov declared: 'We will never see his like again.' Luis Scalise, in his obituary in *Clarín*, wrote: 'He was one of the true greats. And a fascinating character. He won tournaments everywhere and got to be the fifth strongest player in the world. Najdorf was, without doubt, the father of Argentinian chess. His classic pose, with his hands clasped behind his back, will be sorely missed from every competition. From now on, and for ever, Don Miguel is a legend.'

Najdorf himself often said he had no regrets, that he would have chosen the same life if he had to live all over again. 'All I wish is that it could have been 30 years later. Firstly, because when I was born, girls were not wearing mini-skirts, and secondly because chess didn't seem to be such a popular sport and players didn't earn so much money. Today, a Kasparov or a Fischer is a multi-millionaire. And I like the new rate of play. Before the Second World War, it was slow: two and a half hours for 32 moves. Nowadays, the organizers and the sponsors realize that time is more valuable than ever.'

Once, when asked what chess had taught him, he replied: 'I learned how to lose, but I have had a happy life. Chess has given me the strength to go on living. And my finest game is still to come.' ■

Jan Timman

A Healthy Dose of Optimism

On the chessboard, as in life, Miguel Najdorf always looked for the sunny side. Jan Timman played the Argentinian legend seven times. He remembers a player with an enterprising style in which strategy and tactics balanced each other out.

s a chess player, Najdorf is often bracketed together with Reshevsky: two top players who were not from the Soviet Union but from the Americas. There was an obvious difference, however. Reshevsky was a child prodigy who was already playing simuls before Najdorf had even mastered the rules of chess. Najdorf was a late developer. More: he even became a 'greybeard prodigy', a concept thought up by the Dutch writer Harry Mulisch.

Najdorf was born in 1910, a year before Botvinnik, Lilienthal and Reshevsky. I have never played against the former two and only two games against Reshevsky, but I often ran into Najdorf during tournaments. He was still reasonably successful at an advanced age, and we played each other seven times.

Najdorf was also a striking presence in the social sphere because of his conversational skills. Despite the more than 40-year age difference, we

got on extremely well. I have many cherished memories of the dinners with him and the countless bottles of red wine we put away in Buenos Aires, Mar del Plata and Bugojno.

Najdorf had an enterprising playing style in which strategy and tactics balanced each other out. He was also helped by a healthy dose of optimism. A typical example was his comment after his defeat of Botvinnik in the final round of the Staunton tournament of 1946. According to the tournament book, Najdorf maintained that he had already been winning on move 9, and that he only had to prove it. Yet it was a normal opening position that the computer assesses as equal.

Najdorf scored his greatest successes after World War II, but even before that time he had been a strong player. After deciding to remain in Buenos Aires in 1939 he played his first tournament there immediately after the Olympiad. It had been organized by the club Circulo de Ajedrez. Najdorf shared first place with Keres after annihilating his rival in their personal encounter.

SL 10.13 – D94
Miguel Najdorf
Paul Keres
Buenos Aires 1939

1.d4 d5 2.c4 c6 3.e3 ♘f6 4.♘f3 g6 5.♗d3 ♗g7 6.0-0 0-0 7.♘c3 dxc4 8.♗xc4

8...♘bd7 The modern move is 8...♗g4, to allow for quick piece development. **9.♕e2 ♘e8** Black's opening is anything but impressive, which is surprising. Keres had been a correspondence player in his youth and usually played excellent openings. Najdorf didn't regard the text as bad – he played it himself against Bolbochan 10 years later. **10.♗b3 e5 11.♘xe5 ♘xe5 12.dxe5 ♗xe5**

13.f4

Enterprising play. White establishes absolute dominance in the centre.

13...♗g7

The computer prefers 13...♗xc3, but it seems to me that very few people would be willing to voluntarily give up their bishop pair in this way.

14.e4

14...♗e6

In order to relieve the pressure, Black allows his pawn structure to be weakened. Najdorf will exploit this to the full.

15.♗xe6 fxe6 16.e5 ♘c7 17.♗e3 ♘d5 18.♘e4 b6 19.♖ad1 ♕e7 20.g3 ♖ad8

21.a3 A quiet move to underline the superiority of White's position.

21...♘c7

Black wants to swap rooks in order to alleviate the pressure, but this plan runs into a tactical refutation.

22.♖d6 First the rook penetrates.

22...c5 Now Black is ready for 22...♘b5, after which his problems would be solved. But White now strikes a hammer blow.

23.f5!

A sharply calculated breakthrough that wins by force.

23...exf5 24.♗g5 ♕xe5 25.♗xd8 ♘e6 26.♗f6!

A beautiful final move. Black resigns, since after 26...♗xf6 27.♘xf6+ he will be a rook down.

During the match between the Soviet Union and the Rest of the World in 1970, Najdorf made a name for himself by beating Tal in a sensational game. Possibly even more famous is his win against Fischer in Santa Monica four years before that. Starting from a Benoni-like set-up he succeeded in outplaying Fischer strategically.

Najdorf was used to playing all kinds of positions, and he played many different openings. In the Sicilian, for example, he played not only the line named after him, but also the Rauzer and the Scheveningen.

He could be impressive in his way of handling the Benoni.

BI 5.13 – A65
Boris Ivkov
Miguel Najdorf
Havana ol 1966 (5)

1.d4 ♘f6 2.c4 g6 3.♘c3 c5 4.d5 ♗g7 5.e4 d6 6.♗d3 0-0 7.♘ge2 e6 8.0-0 exd5 9.cxd5 ♖e8 10.♘g3 ♘a6 11.h3 ♘c7

A somewhat unusual move order has given rise to a well-known line of the Benoni.

11...♘c7

Jan Timman and Miguel Najdorf at the 1978 Olympiad in Buenos Aires. 'Despite the more than 40-year age difference, we got on extremely well.'

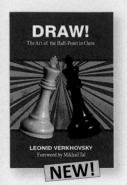
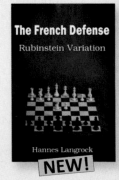

12.♗f4 The most common continuation is 12.a4. It indeed makes sense to first play a move that will have to be played anyway, and only then decide what square to develop the white queen's bishop to. Sometimes it's a good idea to put the bishop on g5, followed by an advance of the f-pawn.

12...a6 13.a4 ♖b8 The usual plan in the Benoni: Black is aiming for ...b7-b5.

14.a5 Trying to put a spanner in Black's works.

14...b5
Another standard Benoni move. Black advances the b-pawn regardless in order to create counterplay along the half-open b-file.

15.axb6 ♖xb6

16.♘a4
The question is whether the knight is well positioned at the edge. The alternative 16.♕d2 offered better chances of an opening advantage.

16...♖b7
The best square for the rook. Black wants to double rooks on the e-file, if possible.

17.♖b1 ♘b5 18.b4
Too energetic. Correct was 18.♖e1 in order to provide extra cover for the e-pawn.

18...c4!
With this advance Black secures an advantage. White cannot really capture the pawn, as this will lose the e-pawn and put paid to all coordination in the white camp.

19.♗c2 ♘d7
With 19...♘a3 Black could have secured the bishop pair, also with a positional advantage. But Najdorf wants the preserve all the position's dynamic possibilities.

20.♘e2 ♘e5 21.♗c1

21...♕h4!
What Najdorf does here is a classic

example of how to play the Benoni. Black is aiming for optimum activity for his pieces.

22.f4 ♘d7 23.♗b2

White decides to force a strategically desirable exchange of bishops, but it will not be enough to contain the black initiative.

23...♗xb2

Very correct. In these cases it is better to swap yourself than to allow your opponent to do so, since the black king would be less well-placed on g7.

24.♖xb2 ♘f6 25.♘ac3

White understandably wants to swap his miserable knight for Black's mighty steed, but now things go wrong for him tactically. But it would have been hard to suggest a useful alternative anyway.

25...♘xc3 26.♘xc3

26...♗xh3! A hammer blow. 27.gxh3 will be met decisively by 27...♕g3+.

27.♕d4

27...♗f5!

A spectacular move that leaves White with a hopeless position. There is no effective defence against the threat of 28...♘g4.

28.♗b1 ♘g4 29.g3 ♕xg3+ 30.♖g2 ♕h3 31.exf5 ♘e3 32.♗e4

32...♖be7 The computer considers 32...♖xb4 even stronger, but the text is more principled: Black had already prepared for this doubling of rooks 17 moves ago.

33.♖ff2 ♘xg2 34.♖xg2 ♕h4 35.♖f2

35...f6!

An accurate final move. White resigned. A remarkably sprightly game for a 56-year-old! ■

Discover what kind of player you really are!

In this first of a series of instructional articles, **Parimarjan Negi** compares chess to video games. As you aim to improve your game you should choose the avatars that suit you. In a brief tour of chess history the Indian grandmaster shows that you are not the first to embark on that journey.

The purpose of computation is insight, not numbers – Richard Hamming

I used to suck at math in high school. Actually, I still suck at math. But back then, I couldn't see the point in studying those abstract number 'tricks'. I would learn the inexplicable formulas, apply a couple of them to pointless problems, and then promptly forget about them.

Now, as a freshman at Stanford, I see math pop up everywhere. It drives me to try to grasp the bigger picture – the history and need behind the mathematical inventions – and suddenly I find it easier to learn. The formulas might still be intimidating, but I can sense a structure to them. And I don't have to be very good at it to learn something new and useful.

So what's the idea behind chess? I feel it's an ancient video game – a precursor to this branch of modern multi-player games, or e-sports.

At first, this might seem an ironic comparison. Chess can be painfully slow. League of Legends (a game that I see my dorm mates obsess about all day) is full of flashing lights, blasts, magic, kills, and what not. Chess is considered purely intellectual, League sounds more like a teenage addiction.

But beyond these differences, the underlying purposes are the same. They are both a portal to a virtual world of extensive strategy.

Compared to the video games, it's the rustic nature of chess that is its greatest strength. It's like the difference between books and movies. Everything is more subtle, yet more involved. You create your own world – and it's different every time. In your mind, it can be more violent and ferocious than any game could ever be. But it can also be a place of peace and meditation.

In the video games, you choose and develop your virtual avatar. But in chess, the lines between you and your avatar as a player are far more blurred. We hear about players being attacking or defensive, artists or scientists. Romanticists or realists. But this is just a part of your chess identity – it's really about the fusion of your real self and your imagined self, your skills and weaknesses, in one complex evolving web. After all, playing is not just about the lines you calculate, but also about the decisions you make. And the ones you don't.

A player's style evolves constantly – and in a circular fashion. You learn the value of the pieces, then you learn the value of sacrificing them. You learn the art of defending, which in turn leads to learning how to refine an initiative. And so on. Every time you master something, you'll face better players who will make you re-learn the very topics again.

That's why we study the classical games – because this process imitates the historical evolution of the chess styles. Those champions created these techniques in response to the very same difficulties that we face today while improving. To improve, you don't have to find their moves, but understand the concept behind their styles so you can adapt it to your level.

To illustrate this, I'll make a parallel between this and the development of a kid's chess style (mine, as I can only explain my own thinking properly). I have simplified things and focused only on particular aspects of their styles to paint a bigger picture.

A few pages won't drastically alter your understanding, but hopefully, when you study the classics yourself in greater depth, this will help you absorb it better. After all, understanding an idea begins with appreciating it.

In the earliest days of chess, people experimented around with and figured out the relative values for the pieces. The next step was the era of Philidor (1726-95), who, among other things, studied the endgames. And they were really complex ones to develop from scratch – for instance, I actually did not find the win in the most famous of these (♖ + ♗ vs ♖) even after I had become a GM and despite having seen it countless times before. Obviously I didn't start studying such things until much later, but the idea was similar. Reduce the complexity – the unexpected moving parts in a position – to the minimum, see the way pieces interact in such settings, and suddenly you understand their power better.

Next, you learn a few more rules and tricks – centre, development, castle, fork, pin, and you are able to play decent chess. It's not terribly exciting – you count material, try to save your pieces, attack his pieces. That's how it was before the romanticists of the 19th century realized what you could gain by chasing your opponent's king without caring about the material!

1. Morphy-Anderssen
Paris 1858 (9)

7...f5 In the style of those days, Black plays aggressively. **8.♘1c3!** Development! **8...f4 9.♘d5 fxe3 10.♘bc7+**

♔f7 **11.♕f3+ ♘f6 12.♗c4 ♘d4 13.♘xf6+ d5 14.♗xd5+ ♔g6 15.♕h5+ ♔xf6 16.fxe3 ♘xc2+ 17.♔e2**

Black resigned. A perfectly aesthetic attack on the king! All White's moves were natural and flowed smoothly. At the same time, he did not require a lot of subtlety in the attack.

Of course Morphy was more than just blindly chasing the king – his games had a lot of subtlety as well, and that is what allowed him to execute his attacks with such effortless ease... If only his opponents had challenged him more, perhaps we might have seen him invent even different styles of play. But this kind of play is one of the first impulses as a player's chess style begins to take shape. At least, for me it was:

2. Sanka-Negi
Tehran 2002 (8)

Looking at this game now, it seems pretty simple and unimpressive, but it had a big impact on me back when I played it: **18...g3! 19.♗xa7** Or 19.hxg3 fxg3 20.♗xg3 h4, followed by ...♘h5, ♘gf4, ♕g5. The attack continues. **19...♘xd5 20.♘xe5 ♗xe5 21.♕xd5+ ♔h8 22.♗c4 ♕h4 23.h3 ♖xa7** Unnecessary, but I guess I just liked making extra sacrifices ☺. **24.♘xa7**

24...♗xh3! 25.gxh3 ♕xh3 26.♕d2 ♘h4 ...g3-g2, and mate followed soon.

I had lost my previous three games against Sanka. I had never won a major title in my life. This game changed all that – and more. It brought about a huge shift in my

> 'I remember the feeling of pure invincibility. It feels like you can breach any defence.'

chess personality – surging my belief. I remember the feeling of pure invincibility. It's like when you know a secret. It feels like you can breach any defence. Material and other such things seem to be pointless. Chess seems to have only one objective: go for the king.

Of course, it's important to note the big difference between the development of my style and Morphy's.

I wasn't creating anything – I saw games of countless World Champions, I saw brilliant attacking examples, as well as defensive examples. I was inundated with information. Yet, I couldn't just start playing in the style of Lasker, or Fischer, despite seeing their games. My style had to be developed slowly, which, despite all this knowledge that was at hand, was a process of discovery and realization in its own right.

3. Chigorin-Steinitz
Havana 1889 (15)

12...♕b8 It's an ugly, ugly position for Black. Remember there was no real theory at that time, and experimenting in the opening could land you into serious trouble. Throughout this game, White's play could be improved upon, and Black was lost on multiple occasions. But it's easy to say all that with engines running and our modern understanding and accuracy – White's moves, although not particularly subtle, certainly made sense. **13.♗xe7 ♔xe7 14.d6+ ♔f8 15.♘xe5 f6 16.♘f3**

16...♗c5! Getting some notion of counterplay. **17.e5 b5 18.♗xb5**

cxb5 **19.♘xb5 ♘e6 20.exf6 gxf6 21.♕h4 ♔f7 22.♕h5+ ♔g8 23.♕g4+ ♔f7 24.♕h5+ ♔g7** White still has to show some accuracy, despite his overwhelming position.

25.♘fd4 ♗xd4 26.♘xd4 ♖f8

27.♖d3 White had other ways to win, but this rook lift is the most natural one. **27...♗b7! 28.♘xe6+ dxe6 29.♖h3 ♗e4 30.♕g4+ ♗g6**

Suddenly the tables have turned completely! It's impressive to see how, despite taking so many punches, Black kept clinging on to the slightest chances. (0-1, 36)

A cold shower for the attacker! Some people can just dig deep, calculate, and prevent your mating attacks. It took me a while, and some painful defeats, to get to that realization. For some reason, I vividly remember the following one:

4. Negi-Shetty
Mumbai 2004 (8)

It's a normal position, and I could do a lot of different things, but instead I started obsessively trying to find a mate. **18.f6 ♘xd3**

19.g6?? It's hard for me now to even imagine what I was thinking here. I remember calculating 19...hxg6 20.fxg7 ♔xg7 21.♖xf7+ as a beautiful win, so I just had to play this. Almost everything else just allows Black to defend everything and win, of course. **19...♘xf6 20.gxf7+ ♔xf7 21.cxd3 ♕c8** and Black soon won.

As you can see, I was somewhat one-dimensional in my hunger to go after the king. Some people start out differently – actually preferring endgames or slow manoeuvring (seriously, they do exist, or so I have been told). So of course the historical evolution of the chess styles matching a player's own evolution is too general, and probably doesn't apply often. But, as your style develops, you can definitely find historical precedents, the reasons and need for such a style to have been created – and I feel that this context might just give the process a little push.

Note that Steinitz wasn't just a great defender. He built those skills on top of the attacking skills that were largely prevalent in his era. You can't be a great player by just relying on one set of skills. Look at the following game in which the players' roles are reversed:

5. Steinitz-Chigorin
Havana 1892 (4)

20.♕f1!? An interesting way to bring in the queen. I wonder if he already saw ideas like the one executed in the game? **20...a5 21.d4 exd4 22.♘xd4 ♗xd4**

23.♖xd4!? A devilish idea... **23...♘xd4 24.♖xh7+! ♔xh7 25.♕h1+ ♔g7 26.♗h6+ ♔f6 27.♕h4+ ♔e5 28.♕xd4+** and mate follows.

The next era of players – Lasker, Rubinstein, Capablanca, Nimzowitsch, Réti, just to name a few, were really the ones who laid down the groundwork of chess strategy. All those positional ideas that we often hear about were largely developed by them. It was an incredible period of a new type of chess – these guys showed that we could win without doing anything flashy, and by playing very simple and sensible chess as well. Also, endgames were absolutely transformed in this period. These guys showed again and again that apparently drawish (read: equal material) endgames had a lot of life left in them. They developed the art of 'outplaying' an opponent, slowly but surely.

6. Lasker-Rubinstein
St Petersburg 1914

An extremely drawish endgame between two of the best endgame experts of that generation. Lasker executes the rook-behind-the-passed-pawn concept perfectly, while Rubinstein completely underestimates it... An important landmark in the development of an idea that is completely taken for granted these days. **52.♖f1 ♔d6 53.g4 hxg4 54.hxg4**

54...c5? Black's chances would have been much better with the bishops remaining on the board. **55.dxc5+ ♗xc5 56.♗xc5+ ♔xc5 57.f5 gxf5 58.gxf5**

Black definitely has defensive chances if we analyse the position carefully,

but it's obviously not very easy. Here, Rubinstein tries to play the obvious defensive moves, but his position instantly collapses. **58...♖f6 59.♖f4 b4 60.b3**

That's why a rook in front of the pawn sucks. Black has to give the king entry or allow White to advance his pawn even further. **60...♖f7 61.f6 ♔d6 62.♔d4 ♔e6 63.♖f2! ♔d6 64.♖a2 ♖c7 65.♖a6+ ♔d7 66.♖b6** Black resigned. He is unable to defend his remaining pawns. An amazing display of technique. Such rook manoeuvres would be obvious nowadays, but remember this was the time when they were developing them from scratch.

I remember the time when I first became obsessed with a preference for bishops over knights after studying some of these games. The feeling when I started winning such slow games was a whole different kind of satisfaction – I was still mostly a rather blunt kind of player, but the idea of forcing your opponent into submission was new and appealing.

7. Pahm Minh Duc-Negi
Heraklio 2002

28...♗d5 29.♔e3 f5! Pushing all the pawns. Of course, the assessment should be equal, but we were 9-year-old kids, and somehow it felt as if I was outplaying him, despite all the help he gave me.

30.g3 e5 31.f4 ♔f6 32.a3 g5 33.b4 cxb4 34.cxb4 h5 I guess pushing all your pawns can just be scary for your opponent in the under-10 category. Finally he collapsed:

35.h4? exf4+ 36.gxf4 gxh4 37.♘f1 ♔e6 38.♔d4 ♔d6 and eventually I found a way to penetrate with my king and win.

Although I must admit that I didn't learn these lessons particularly well, I was able to outplay my 2000 level opponents by showing Capablancanesque technique as in the game above, but when I reached higher levels, for a long time I made little progress when trying to do the same. This clearly shows how ideas and techniques from great players can be implemented at your own level even if you don't fully grasp their play. And how even in your own games, these need to constantly evolve as you get better.

Possibly, Alekhine signified the return of the attackers. Of course, as you saw in the Steinitz game above, every strong player was very much capable of building a powerful attack. But Alekhine integrated the strategic elements to create a much more nuanced understanding of initiative, compensation, activity and attack.

8. Selezniev-Alekhine
Triberg 1921

It's been an instructive game so far, where after a lot of complications White seems to have stabilized. But not really: **35...h5!** Adding some pressure. **36.♕c2 h4 37.♕d3 ♖d8 38.f3 ♕h5 39.♕e4 hxg3 40.hxg3 ♕g5 41.♔g2 ♕d2+ 42.♔h3 ♗f6**

Intending ...♔g7 and ...♖h8+. It is quite amazing how Alekhine managed to conjure up such a powerful

attack out of thin air. **43.♖c2 ♕h6+ 44.♔g2 ♔g7 45.g4 ♖h8 46.♔f2**

46...♖b8!? Just mixing the plans – this wasn't particularly required, but surprisingly it is the best move, even according to the modern engine! He continued exerting pressure on both sides and converted the point.

The next generation produced many great personalities – from the methodical Euwe and Botvinnik to the flamboyant Tal. There were improved versions of Alekhine's attacking genius in players such as Stein and Spassky, while yet many others introduced more refined styles of the strategic masters. But everyone appeared to have a distinct style and speciality.

That's why I feel the next huge shift in chess personalities was brought about by Fischer. His was a universal style – integrating everything before him, and taking all elements – theory, initiative, endgame – to the highest level. There were attempts to find the objective truth in the position – an idea very common nowadays among the best players, largely due to the incredibly high standards set by the computers. But he did it all without any such external influence, which is what makes his style so ground-breaking. Studying the evolution of his game from the early years to his peak would be the most daunting, and rewarding, of experiences in itself.

The generation after Fischer saw the rise of an increasing amount of great universal players... but let's just fast forward to the present.

Compared to the past, everyone has to have ridiculously deep and excellent opening preparation. Due to the engines, the standards in all aspects of the game – attack or defence, endgames or complications – are so much higher. Above all, you have to be consistent. Producing an occasional brilliancy isn't enough to make an impact – you have to be able to do it repeatedly. You might think that such requirements would just force each player to be almost indistinguishable from the other, right?

True, they are good at everything. But the way they go about implementing their skills is still very personal, very unique to each.

Carlsen is a psychologist. He understands a secret of chess – that sometimes, however well you play and calculate, if a freak, brilliant tactic ruins your position, you're dead. So he's always in control – he'll first prevent your counterplay, and then go about improving his position. Of course, when he's pushed against the wall, particularly with black, he can just as easily enter unexpected complications, but no more than he needs to. He doesn't try to play the best move in the position, but the best move against the opponent. At the same time, he does whatever needs to be done – never getting hung on to emotional aspects of the position such as its aesthetics, or how the position was two moves back.

9. Svidler-Carlsen
London 2013

In the post-game press conference, Magnus was asked if he had considered 25...♗xh3, which, according to the engines, seems to yield a large advantage. Apparently, he thought it was too risky to go for such complications here, because he could get a safe edge without it. If there had not been any other way to get an advantage, I am sure he'd have definitely considered 25...♗xh3 a lot more seriously, but here his pragmatic choice worked perfectly: **25...exd3 26.♗xd3 ♗xd3 27.♖xd3 c5 28.♗e5 ♖xd3 29.♗xb8**

29...c4! White's position doesn't seem bad. Certainly not as bad as it could have been after 25...♗xh3 – after all, everything is equal, right? Yet White now loses almost without a struggle (partly because of time-pressure, but also because it's really tough to play without being able to create much in the way of counterplay). **30.♗e5 ♗c5 31.♖b1 ♕d5 32.♖b8+ ♔h7 33.♕h5 ♕e4 34.♖b2 ♖d5 35.♖e2 ♕b1+ 36.♔h2 f6** and White resigned.

Caruana doesn't seem to notice his opponent at all. Perhaps that's why he's one of the toughest rivals for Carlsen – because he seems impervious to the psychology that haunts most of us.

When we calculate, we waste a whole lot of time just repeating the same lines, or just losing ourselves in abstractions. But he seems to be able to do these calculations most efficiently – and then chase an objective gold standard – precision, precision, precision.

10. Anand-Caruana
Moscow 2013 (1)

Caruana's a pawn down, although the two bishops obviously give him compensation. Here he completely switches modes and plays the aggressive **20... g5!**, creating all sorts of threats for White. **21.♘h2** But now he doesn't press on with the plan to get a strong initiative, but instead makes use of an important change in the position.

21...♖d8!
Since the ♘f3 has moved, ...g4 is no longer much good, so Black switches to calm play, utilizing his bishop pair and active pieces. **22.d4 exd4 23.cxd4 ♗b4 24.♖e2 ♕xd4 25.♘df1**

25...♕c5! Another slightly surprising, but brutally precise shift. Exchanging the queens makes Black's active pieces even more prominent. White could certainly have defended better, but Black's execution proceeded with clinical precision. **26.♕xc5 ♗xc5 27.♖c2 ♗d6 28.♘g4 ♔g7 29.♗d2 ♔g6 30.♘ge3 f5 31.♘c4 ♘xc4 32.♖xc4 ♖a8 33.♖c1 f4 34.♗c3 h5 35.♘d2 ♗d5 36.f3 ♗c5+ 37.♔f1 ♗e3 38.♔e2 ♗c4+ 39.♔e1 ♖e8 40.♔d1 ♗xd2 41.♔xd2 ♖e2+ 42.♔d1 ♖xg2** and White soon resigned.

But the most remarkable chess styles at the top are those of Aronian and Grischuk. They are artists. As you get better, your natural instinct is to play beautiful moves, and there are many

strong players whose creativity seems to have no bounds. But it's amazing to be able to do this at the very top – of course, they don't create something aesthetic in every game, but every now and then you see them sculpt something that is simply beautiful. I can't imagine Carlsen choosing a line just because of its beauty, but with these two, I'm sure it happens often.

'The most remarkable chess styles at the top are those of Aronian and Grischuk. They are artists.'

16.d5! cxd5 17.♘xd5 ♕c5+ 18.♘ce3! fxe3 19.b4!

The previous moves were just amazing. They aren't so hard to calculate, but the very fact that they work so well is what is so astounding. And to be able to play such moves, you need to perceive this long beforehand. Now it's all done: **19...♕d6 20.♖xe3 ♘a6 21.♗b2 ♗g7 22.♘f6+** Black resigned.

Nowadays, looking at the computer screen, one gets the impression that good and bad moves are as simple as Black and White. This is perhaps the greatest risk you face while trying to get better these days, because chess can be played in many ways. The objective level of an engine is just an abstraction, but in a game between mere mortals, the truth doesn't matter. What matters is the process by which you decide your moves, and its internal consistency with your personality as a chess player.

So take a moment to consider what chess means to you. Imagine your own world inside the game. And make it more vivid. ■

11. Aronian-Popov
Moscow 2005 (4)

White could continue in many simple ways, but he goes for the exciting and incalculable **9.♘xb5 cxb5 10.♗xb5+ ♔f8 11.0-0.**

This position can be analysed in great depth, but what I want you to notice is the harmonious way in which White develops his compensation here. Everything seems to proceed smoothly in a perfectly beautiful set of moves. **11...♗a6 12.a4 ♘e4 13.♘d3 ♗b7 14.f3 ♘f6 15.♘e5 ♕c7 16.♗d2 h5 17.c6 ♗c8 18.e4 ♕b6 19.♗e3 ♗e6 20.♖ac1 ♘a6 21.f4! ♘c7** On 21...♘xe4, 22.♕xd5! is the idea. **22.f5 gxf5 23.exf5 ♗c8 24.♖c5!**

Amazingly, the computer still considers Black to be better. Who knows; it might even be right, but it's incredibly tough to play when your opponent is constantly playing such aesthetic moves. In the game, Black began to collapse here: **24...♗a6 25.♗g5 ♗c8 26.♔h1 ♘e4 27.♗xe7+! ♔xe7 28.♖xd5 ♘xd5 29.♕xd5 ♘g5 30.♘g6+ fxg6 31.♖e1+** and mate follows.

12. Grischuk-Rodshtein
Bilbao 2014 (3)

In this game, Grischuk played quite creatively from the start in a typical but unexplored Réti side-line. Now he starts punishing Black with powerful play – notice again how all White's pieces come together right when they are needed. **14.g4 f4 15.g5 ♘h5**

A happy crowd of chess players is showered with confetti at the end of the 2014 SportAccord Mind Games. No doubt many of them will return to Beijing for the next edition.

GU XIAOBING

Grischuk and Hou Yifan excel in Mind Games

Once again the end of the year saw a great number of players eager to spend large amounts of their time at a board travel to Beijing for the SportAccord World Mind Games. The action comprised bridge, go, xiangqi, draughts, and chess. And yes, the attentive reader is right that you don't need a board to play bridge, but as most chess players love to play cards (including Pineapple Open-Face Chinese Poker!), let's not discriminate bridge players! Taking part for the third time, **Maxime Vachier-Lagrave** is beginning to feel like a regular in the Chinese capital. Our reporter played a prominent part in all three competitions, but the star in the men's section was Alexander Grischuk, who claimed both the blitz and the rapid. World Champion Hou Yifan showed her class by winning the women's blitz and Basque competitions.

With gold medals in the Rapid and Blitz competitions, Alexander Grischuk was the most successful chess player in Beijing.

S

Some things don't change. Just like last year, the jetlag victims would gather early for breakfast. This time I am delighted to report that Peter Leko decided to join our little group. I also welcomed Etienne Bacrot in Team France, eager to clinch good places and good prizes in rapid, blitz and 'Basque' chess (where you play two games simultaneously against the same opponent, one with white, the other with black). Etienne and I actually played a few training games, mostly in Basque, as I feared this one particular event after my bad experience last year. I was indeed a bit vengeful, as in-between there had also been a disastrous World Rapid & Blitz Championship. I felt it was about time to play properly again.

That said, I had no big expectations for the rapid that we started with, possibly because there is so much time on the clock that I feel like taking a walk and watching the other games. But I am not alone in that respect. Anyway, I didn't have that opportunity in the first game against Ian Nepomniachtchi. He played so fast that I hardly managed to get up from my chair. But sticking to the same speed in the tricky pawn down rook endgame he had to play cost him dearly. While I finished the first day on 50 per cent, Sasha Grischuk was on a very decent +2. However, that was not enough for the lead, as Wang Hao, with 3 fine wins and a draw with Black against Sasha, had had a great start.

After a welcome evening break filled with Pineapple Open-Face Chinese Poker with Etienne and Sasha (despite him beating both of us that day…), which would become a regular daily feature – as said, chess players just love playing cards – it was time to focus on the second day of rapid. On the top board, Wang Hao managed to retain his lead with two draws against Shakh and myself, but Sasha joined him in the lead with a fine win with black against Vassily Ivanchuk, meaning he had won all his Black games, and only his Black games. The situation going into the final round was Sasha and Wang Hao sharing the lead, with no fewer than four players a full point behind them but with a theoretical chance to catch up: Ian, Shakh, Levon and myself. Sasha, as White against Ian, decided not to disrupt his winning strategy – or was it the strength of the Grünfeld once again? – and forced a quick draw. Meanwhile, Levon played a textbook game against Wang Hao's solid Slav.

SL 4.5 – D17
Levon Aronian
Wang Hao
Beijing rapid 2014 (7)

1.♘f3 d5 2.d4 ♘f6 3.c4 c6 4.♘c3 dxc4 5.a4 ♗f5 6.♘e5 ♘bd7 7.♘xc4 ♘b6 8.♘e5 a5 9.f3 ♘fd7 10.♘xd7 ♘xd7 11.e4 ♗g6 12.♗e2

12...e6
Despite the little I know about this line, I think this main move is a bit too passive for rapid play. 12...♕b6 13.f4 e5! might be the way, although Levon no doubt would have improved on his recent game against Csaba Balogh.
13.0-0 ♗b4 14.♗e3 0-0 15.♕b3 ♕c7 16.♔h1 ♖ad8 17.♖ac1 ♕b8

18.♗g1
This is a mysterious over-protecting move. I think Levon was just trying to get Wang Hao into time-trouble. There was nothing wrong with the immediate 18.♖fd1 ♗d6 19.g3.
18...♖fe8 19.♖fd1 ♗d6
19...e5 20.d5 is unfortunately never an option.
But 19...f6! was called for, to bring the bishop back into play: 20.♗c4 ♗f7 21.♗f2 ♘b6 22.♗e2 ♘d7 23.♗g3 ♕a7, and White has only a slight edge.
20.♗c4

20...h5
I don't like this move. Pseudo-active moves in rapid play generally end up creating weaknesses instead of real counterplay.
21.♘e2 ♕c7 22.♗e3 ♖c8

23.♗d2! Now I like this plan, giving as little counterplay as possible.
23...♖a8 24.♕e3 f6 25.♘f4
Black's position is horrible.
25...♗xf4
25...♗f7 26.♘d3 ♘b6 27.♗b3 ♘d7 28.f4 is not an option, as White's pieces will one by one reach their ideal squares, while Black can only wait for White's action on the kingside.
26.♕xf4 ♕xf4 27.♗xf4

In a classical game, White would enjoy all the free play and Black would face a long and tough defence. In rapid, he simply doesn't have time to find a solution to his problems.
27...♗f7 28.♗e3
Avoiding any ...e5.

28...♘b8 After 28...f5! 29.e5 ♘b6

30.♗b3 ♘d5 31.♗g5 Black probably has one too many holes in his position. Still, closing the centre is the natural way of defending here.
29.♔g1 ♘a6 30.♗e2 ♘b4 31.♗f4! ♖ed8
31...♖e7 32.♗d6 ♖d7 33.♗c5 would have boiled down to the same thing.
32.♗c7 ♖d7 33.♗b6

With very simple means, White has rendered Black's position completely hopeless: a5 will fall.
33...♘a6 34.♗xa5 ♘b8 35.b4 e5

36.d5! The rest is easy.
36...♔h7 37.♗c4 ♘a6 38.h4 ♔g6 39.♔h2 ♗g8 40.♗d3 ♘b8 41.f4 exf4 42.d6
Not the cleanest, but a breakthrough is a breakthrough!
42...♗b3 43.♖d2 ♔f7 44.♖c3 ♗e6 45.♗c2 ♘a6 46.b5 cxb5 47.axb5 ♘c5 48.♗c7 b6 49.♖xc5
And a nice touch to finish it.
49...bxc5 50.b6 Black resigned.

That meant a first gold medal for Sasha. Both Shakh and I won our last-round game, and I have the pleasure to share my aesthetic and completely unnecessary king march against Peter.

Maxime Vachier-Lagrave treated Peter Leko to 'an aesthetic and completely unnecessary king march'.

Vachier-Lagrave-Leko
Beijing rapid 2014 (7)

I used my whole three minutes to come up with the bold **51.♔d4+?** not seeing that my king could easily go downwards to safety! 51.♗f2, followed by 52.♔d2, was curtains.
51...♔f7 52.♔c5 ♕xb2

53.♖ee3 It was difficult to see 53.♕xb7+! ♔g6 54.f5+ ♔h7 55.♔d6!

♕xc3 56.♗e5, but it was already the simplest option available.
53...♘a6+ If 53...♘d3+ then 54.♔d4! ♘c1 55.♗e5!.
54.♔d6 ♕b4+ 55.♔d7
Not altogether reassuring. This journey may have cost me a few minutes of my life...

55...♕f8? While trying to find a decent way to play after 55...c5, Peter ended up playing this move, which got my heart rate back to normal. The cold shower was 55...♗f3!. Although, White has a miraculous, forced and not too difficult win: 56.f5 ♗g4 57.♖f3! ♕e7+ 58.♔c8, and wins. Interesting was 55...c5!? 56.♖e7+ ♔g8 (56...♔g6 57.f5+ ♔xf5 58.♖e5+! ♔g4 59.♖xd5 ♕xc3 60.♕b6! ♔xg3 61.♕g6+ ♔f2 62.♖f5+ ♔e2 63.♕g2+ winning) 57.♕a8+ ♔h7

ANALYSIS DIAGRAM

58.♕f8 (the queen gets out of trouble before White's king shuts her down on a8!) 58...♗c6+ 59.♔c8 ♕xc3 60.♕f5+ ♔h8 61.♖f7!, and yes, White is the one mating!
56.♕xb7 ♘c5+ 57.♖xc5 ♕xc5 58.♖e5 ♕c3 59.♕b8 ♔g6 60.f5+ ♔h7 61.♖e8
Black resigned.

That yielded me a nice tie for 2nd-5th place and actually a silver medal, according to the tiebreaks. Still, one

feels that Wang Hao, who had to settle for bronze, would have deserved it more, as he had been in the lead throughout the event.

And now the winner's best achievement according to the French squad.

SL 6.1 – D31
Etienne Bacrot
Alexander Grischuk
Beijing rapid 2014 (2)

1.d4 d5 2.c4 e6 3.♘c3 c6 4.e3 ♘d7 5.♕c2 ♘h6

Sasha's latest idea, trying to implement ...f5 safely.
6.e4 The principled answer. White lost a tempo in the process, but the knights on d7 and h6 are not looking too bright.
6...e5!
6...dxe4 7.♗xh6 gxh6 8.♕xe4 gives White an edge.
7.♘f3 exd4 8.♘xd4 dxc4 9.♘f3
9.♗xh6!? gxh6 10.0-0-0 ♕g5+ 11.♔b1 ♘b6 gives White very good compensation. But I'd find it hard to give up the two bishops so needlessly.
9...b5 10.a4 ♗b4 11.♗e2 ♘c5

12.♗xh6 More precise was 12.0-0! 0-0 13.axb5 ♗xc3 14.♗e3! because of this delightful intermezzo: 14...♘e6 (14...♗b4? is met by 15.♕xc4; 14...♗b3 15.♖ad1 ♕f6 16.bxc6! is very good for White) 15.♖fd1 ♕f6 16.bxc3 cxb5 17.♖d5, with a clear white advantage.
12...gxh6 13.0-0 0-0 14.axb5 ♗xc3 15.♕xc3 cxb5

White retains excellent compensation for the pawn, and while watching this game, I felt Etienne had great chances to win here.
16.♕e5 ♕b6 17.♖fd1 All seriously natural, but here I would prefer 17.♖a3!. **17...f6 18.♕f4** Bad is 18.♕g3+?! ♔h8 19.♖d6 ♕b7.
18...♗b7 Black's moves are all forced. Although they're not too difficult in themselves, you need a seriously cool mind to feel you'll survive here... **19.♖d6 ♕c7 20.♘d4 a6**

21.f3?! Slow. After 21.♖d1 ♗xe4 22.♘e6 ♘xe6 23.♕xe4 ♘g5 White has compensation but no more. 21.♘f5? runs into 21...♘xe4.
21...♖ad8 22.♘f5 ♖xd6 23.♘xd6 ♗c8 Black is suddenly very safe and White must think about equalizing. And that is an option he may not have!

GU XIAOBING

Our reporter MVL, Etienne Bacrot and Alexander Grischuk are making plans for the evening. Anyone for Pineapply Open-Face Chinese Poker?

24.♖d1 ♗e6
24...♘a4 25.e5 fxe5 26.♕xe5 ♕g7 seemed a bit better. But it's natural to consolidate first.

25.♕xh6? 25.e5! was a must.
25...♘a4 26.e5 ♕c5+
Too late. And Black's conversion was up to par. An amazing turnaround. Even though White didn't have a large advantage, he certainly had a tremendous initiative.
27.♔f1 ♕xe5 28.f4 ♕e3 29.♖e1 ♘xb2 30.♘f5 ♗xf5 31.♗xc4+ ♘xc4 32.♖xe3 ♘xe3+ 33.♔e2 ♘d5 34.♔f3 ♗g6 35.h4 ♖c8 36.h5 ♗f5 37.g4 ♖c3+ 38.♔e2 ♗xg4+ 39.♔d2 ♗f5 40.♔d1 b4
White resigned.

The women's event I followed less closely, mostly because it was taking place at the same time and because keeping up with my own results was complicated enough! In the end Valentina Gunina made it two gold medals for team Russia after winning a decisive game in Round 6 against the bookmakers' favourite, Hou Yifan.

Hou recovered with a win in the final round and clinched silver, while Ushenina finished 3rd on tiebreak.

The awarding ceremony completed the day, and as Russia had also done well in draughts, I now know the Russian anthem better than La Marseillaise!

	Beijing rapid 2014			
1	Alexander Grischuk	RUS 2828	5	2762
2	Maxime Vachier-Lagrave	FRA 2728	4½	2768
3	Wang Hao	CHN 2719	4½	2766
4	Levon Aronian	ARM 2813	4½	2749
5	Shakhriyar Mamedyarov	AZE 2739	4½	2778
6	Ian Nepomniachtchi	RUS 2801	4	2743
7	Vassily Ivanchuk	UKR 2811	4	2746
8	Wang Yue	CHN 2765	3½	2726
9	Boris Gelfand	ISR 2719	3½	2742
10	Leinier Dominguez	CUB 2763	3	2740
11	Peter Leko	HUN 2773	3	2750
12	Radoslaw Wojtaszek	POL 2684	2½	2767
13	Etienne Bacrot	FRA 2731	2½	2761
14	Ruslan Ponomariov	UKR 2738	2½	2747
15	Pentala Harikrishna	IND 2701	2½	2771
16	Teimour Radjabov	AZE 2776	2	2753
	16 players, 7 rounds			

The blitz event was packed with action and as there were no breaks, it was impossible to keep up with all the results. Much to my surprise, I discovered that most of my wins that day had happened after long endgame grinds. Overall, my play was a bit uneven, but 6/10 kept me 1 point behind a pack of three leaders: Ivanchuk, Aronian and a still undefeated Peter Leko, who had beaten me to end my day on a sour note.

The second day went much more to my taste, with first an important win against Levon.

EO 56.7 – A18
Maxime Vachier-Lagrave
Levon Aronian
Beijing blitz 2014 (11)

1.c4 ♞f6 2.♞c3 e6 3.e4 d5 4.e5 d4 5.exf6 dxc3 6.bxc3 ♛xf6 7.d4 e5 8.♞f3 ♞c6

The latest word in this line.
9.♗g5 ♛g6 10.d5 ♞b8 11.h4 e4
Earlier this year in Norway Chess 11...♞d7?! 12.♗d3 e4 13.h5! ♛f5?!

ANALYSIS DIAGRAM

14.♖h4!, and White was winning, was the course of Grischuk-Aronian.

12.♞d4 ♗d6 13.♗e2

In blitz you unfortunately don't have time to dig into this kind of position, which definitely deserves a lot of consideration. But it is also nice to test your intuition and see if you can come up with decent moves despite the complexity of the problems.
13...h6 14.♗h5 ♛h7 15.♗e3 0-0 16.♞b5 ♞d7 17.♞xd6 cxd6 18.♗f4

18...♖e8?
18...♞e5 19.♗xe5 dxe5 20.0-0 seemed playable to me, and it seems slightly more pleasant to play with white.
19.♗xd6 e3

20.0-0! A simple move, ending any black counterplay for now.

20...♞f6 21.fxe3 ♛e4 22.♖xf6 Played by hand. **22...gxf6 23.♗f4 ♛xc4 24.♛f3** I played all of these moves extremely fast. It is quite my specialty to play a few moves in a row without thinking, and when used properly, it might be my strongest asset in blitz play.

24...♗f5 24...♛e4! prevented a White attack for now, although my centre is still most impressive.
25.♗xh6 ♛e4 26.♛g3+ ♗g6 27.♗f3 ♛e5 28.♗f4 ♛xc3

29.♖b1! Another good series of quick moves, started on move 25. **29...♔h8 30.♖xb7 ♖g8 31.♛f2 ♛d3**

32.♔h2 A bit untimely, but I noticed 32.♛b2 two seconds later...
32...♖ac8 33.♛b2 ♛f5

34.♖xa7?? Down to a few seconds, I grabbed a useless pawn. These are the things our brains do... 34.♗g5 ♔g7 35.e4 ♕e5+ 36.♗xe5 fxe5 37.d6 was curtains. **34...♖c2**

35.♕d4? It's a draw after 35.♕b6 ♗h5 36.♗e4 ♖gxg2+ 37.♗xg2 ♗f3 38.♕d8+ ♔g7 39.♗h6+! ♔xh6 40.♕h8+ ♔g6 41.♕g8+ ♔h5 42.♕h8+. **35...♗h5 36.♗e4** I thought I was back to winning again, but a cold shower was waiting for me...

36...♖f2?? Except it didn't come! 36...♖gxg2+!! 37.♗xg2 ♗f3!, and there is simply no way to avoid mate. **37.♗xf5 ♖fxg2+ 38.♔h3 ♖g1 39.♕xf6+** Black resigned. A bumpy game but crucial for my confidence during the rest of the day!

After a loss to Sasha, again with White, I finished the day well with 5½ points from my last six games. This meant sole first place with 14/20, with Sasha (who had a great day as well with 7½/10) and Vassily one point behind. My lead over Levon and Shakh was even 2½ points. And what about the undefeated Peter? He had the unfortunate idea to keep his streak going until Round 13, and after various jokes from Levon and yours truly, he then lost seven in a row. Only blitz can let us witness such ups and downs!

Ivanchuk had a rough start on the third day with four losses in a row, leaving him out of contention. Things didn't go as planned for me either, and

> **'The winner divided his games in two categories: reasonable but boring, and exciting but awful.'**

two wins in a row in games 23 and 24 were not enough to get me started, as those were my only wins of the day. In the meantime, Sasha had caught up with me in Round 21. The race was still very close, but despite a heroic and lucky save against Sasha in Round 28, I couldn't prevent him from winning a second gold medal with 19½/30. I also didn't realize that due to a very good third day, Teimour Radjabov had almost caught up with me, and thus took bronze with 18, while I finished on 18½.

The winner had mixed feelings about his play. He divided his games in two categories: reasonable but boring, and exciting but awful. Fortunately he could be persuaded to comment on one of his exciting games!

NOTES BY
Alexander Grischuk

KI 77.2 – A50
Alexander Grischuk
Shakhriyar Mamedyarov
Beijing blitz 2014 (20)

Despite winning two tournaments in Beijing, I failed to play a single game that I really like there. However, since Dirk Jan was very stubborn in trying to convince me to comment on a game from Beijing, I chose my blitz game with white against Shakhriyar Mamedyarov, which at least was quite exciting.

1.d4 ♘f6 2.c4 b6
During the game I thought that Shakhriyar had just mixed up which bishop pawn to move, but in fact he played 2...b6 several times in Beijing.
3.♘f3

Definitely not the way to 'refute' 2...b6, but in general blitz is not the best time-control to try to 'refute' rare openings.
3...♗b7 4.g3 g6 5.♗g2 ♗g7 6.0-0 0-0 7.♕c2

7...d6 Now Black gets a bad version of the King's Indian. Much more in the spirit of the position was 7...c5.
8.♘c3 ♘bd7 9.♖d1 ♖e8 10.e4 ♕c8 11.h3 e5 12.d5

As I said, Black has got some mixture of a bad King's Indian (because the bishop on b7 and the rook on e8 are badly placed) and a bad Queen's Indian (because the dark-squared bishops are still on the board). However, in such positions, especially in blitz, the main thing for Black is not to lose heart – which Shakh never does!
12...a5 13.♗e3 h6
It is hard to suggest anything constructive for Black, since he is neither in time to get kingside counterplay nor capable of efficiently stopping the white queenside offensive. So I am not going to comment on the next phase in detail. The most interesting events will begin much later anyway.

14.a3 ♗a6 15.♘d2 ♘h7 16.b4 h5 17.h4 ♘df6 18.f3 ♔h8 19.c5

Now Black's position starts to fall to pieces.
19...bxc5 20.bxc5 dxc5 21.♘a4 ♘d7 22.♖ac1 ♗f8 23.♘xc5 ♘xc5 24.♗xc5 ♗h6 25.♗f2 ♖e7 26.♕c3 f5
After this move the computer evaluation exceeds +3 for White, but how

else can Black create counterplay? To understand the following moves one has to keep in mind that here we both had around 15-20 seconds and would soon start playing on the increment (the time-control was 3+2, so three minutes plus a two-second increment per move).

27.♖c2?! Stronger was 27.f4!.
27...f4 28.♘c4?!

28...♗g7?!

UPCOMING TOURNAMENTS

Missing a chance to get real counterplay: 28...♗xc4 29.♕xc4 fxg3! 30.♗xg3 ♗e3+ 31.♔h1 ♕f8.

29.♘xa5 g5 30.♘c6 ♖e8 31.♘b4 gxh4 32.gxh4 ♗b5

Alexander Grischuk won a crazy blitz game against Shakhriyar Mamedyarov. 'And here, knowing that with an extra queen and bishop I am very strong, Shakh resigned.'

33.♖dc1?!
Fearing the illusory ...♗a4 threat. Obviously, after 33.♕xc7 there is no way for Black to win an exchange.

33...♖g8 34.♕xc7 ♕e8
Now at least Black manages to keep the queens on the board.

35.♔h2 ♗f6 36.♗h3 ♖xa3!

This came as a nasty surprise. Just when I thought I had everything protected and under control, the rook appears out of the blue and causes chaos. Obviously, it is still +4 according to the computer.

37.♖c3
37.♗f5! was strong, but one has to see that 37...♖g7 is met by 38.♕xg7+! (since 38.♕c8 is ineffective due to 38...♖xf3 39.♕xe8+ ♗xe8) 38...♗xg7 (38...♔xg7 39.♕c7+) 39.♖c8.

37...♖a4 38.♘c6
38.♗f5! was the move.

38...♖a2 39.♖1c2
And here 39.♖3c2 ♖a3 40.♗f5!.

39...♖a1

40.♗f5? Finally playing ♗f5, but at the absolutely worst moment possible. White was still winning after 40.♖b3!, but it is easy to get scared of 40...♕g6 41.♖xb5 ♖g1

ANALYSIS DIAGRAM

after which only 42.♕xh7+! ♕xh7 (42...♔xh7 43.♗f5) 43.♗xg1 finishes the game.

40...♖g7 41.♕c8 ♕xc8 42.♗xc8 ♗f1!

43.♗b6 And now, since 43.♗h3 is impossible because of mate in two (43...♗xh3 44.♔xh3 ♖h1 mate), Black gets an almost decisive attack. The next few moves are semi-forced.

43...♗xh4 44.♖c1 ♖g2+ 45.♔h1 ♖aa2 46.♗g1

46...♖gd2??
Here, for the umpteenth time in Beijing 2014, I got lucky. After creating a

huge attack out of nothing, Shakhri-yar simply blunders a piece. After the correct 46...♗f2! 47.♖xf1 ♗xg1 White would have had to find the only way:

ANALYSIS DIAGRAM

48.♖a1!! (48.♔h3? runs into 48...♖h2+ 49.♔xg1 ♘g5) 48...♖ab2 49.♖b1! to save the game. I will let the read-ers speculate about the chances of me finding it with 5 seconds on the clock.
47.♖xf1 Phew! **47...♘g5 48.♘xe5 ♗g3 49.♗f5 h4 50.d6 h3**

51.♘g4 Even without his key bishop Shakhriyar keeps fighting and creates a threat. The naive 51.d7?? would be met by 51...♖h2+ 52.♔xh2 ♖xh2+ 53.♔g1 ♖g2+, with perpetual check.
51...h2 52.♗c5 ♘h3 53.d7 ♔g7 54.e5 ♘g1

This move made me wince, but for-tunately it is not checkmate, and not even a check.
55.♖d3 ♖dc2 56.d8♕
And here, knowing that with an extra queen and bishop I am very strong, Shakh resigned.

▪ ▪ ▪

Unfortunately, there was far too much action to show all of it, but I have to mention the brilliant opening idea (for blitz) that I fell into against Ian.

SI 14.12 – B90
Ian Nepomniachtchi
Maxime Vachier-Lagrave
Beijing blitz 2014 (5)

1.e4 c5 2.♘f3 d6 3.d4 cxd4 4.♘xd4 ♘f6 5.♘c3 a6 6.h3 e5 7.♘de2 h5

8.♘g1!? That was unexpected...
8...b5 9.♘f3 ♗b7 10.♘g5

10...b4?!
10...♘bd7 was OK for Black. But in blitz I didn't like letting White do what he wanted with that knight on g5 pointing at my kingside. In reality, White couldn't do much...

11.♘d5 I thought 11.♗c4 was the idea: 11...bxc3 12.♗xf7+ ♔e7, and 13.0-0 is not so good now because of 13...cxb2 14.♗xb2 ♘xe4.
11...♘xd5

12.♗c4!
And this was a very unpleasant sur-prise! I absolutely hadn't noticed the micro-difference between the two lines. A wonderful idea!
12...♘f6 13.♗xf7+ ♔e7 14.0-0

	Beijing blitz 2014				
1	Alexander Grischuk	IGM	RUS	2819	19½
2	Maxime Vachier-Lagrave	IGM	FRA	2776	18½
3	Teimour Radjabov	IGM	AZE	2715	18
4	Levon Aronian	IGM	ARM	2850	17½
5	Vassily Ivanchuk	IGM	UKR	2720	17
6	Shakhriyar Mamedyarov	IGM	AZE	2866	17
7	Ian Nepomniachtchi	IGM	RUS	2788	17
8	Ruslan Ponomariov	IGM	UKR	2758	15
9	Peter Leko	IGM	HUN	2694	14½
10	Boris Gelfand	IGM	ISR	2757	14½
11	Leinier Dominguez	IGM	CUB	2728	13
12	Wang Hao	IGM	CHN	2693	13
13	Wang Yue	IGM	CHN	2680	12½
14	Pentala Harikrishna	IGM	IND	2728	11½
15	Radoslaw Wojtaszek	IGM	POL	2743	11½
16	Etienne Bacrot	IGM	FRA	2739	10
	16 players, 30 rounds				

White doesn't seem to have much for the piece, but my kingside is completely blocked and his pieces are not easy to repel. In a blitz game it is very difficult to play this position with black.

14...♘c6 14...♘xe4? runs into 15.♗d5, while 14...♕c7 is met by 15.♕f3.

15.a3 a5 16.♗e3

White improves, and I immediately decided to give back some material.

16...g6

17.♗xg6?! Better was 17.♗a2!? ♕c7 18.f4 ♗h6 19.♕d3, with still a lot of initiative on the light squares.

17...♖g8 18.♗f5 ♗c8 18...♘d4! would have been the right way to play. I'm actually quite surprised not to have found this natural move, although I seem to remember that I had noticed it a few moves after playing the text-move. After 19.♗xd4 ♖xg5 20.♗e3 ♖g8 everything should be fine.

19.axb4 ♗xf5 20.exf5

20...axb4? Automatic but bad. Correct was 20...♕c8! 21.♘e6 ♘d8. 20...♘xb4! would also have been OK. But it was clear I needed to shut down the a-file, which I would always have to concede otherwise.

GU XIAOBING

Ian Nepomniachtchi: a brilliant opening idea (for blitz).

21.♘e6?

The move was 21.♕d3!, with a decisive invasion on the light squares to follow.

21...♕c8?

Why I didn't play 21...♖xa1! is another mystery, as I definitely considered this move: 22.♘xd8 ♖xd1 23.♘xc6+ ♔d7 24.♘xe5+ dxe5 25.♖xd1+, and Black is fine if not better!

22.♗g5 ♖xa1 23.♕xa1

23...♕b7

I didn't consider 23...♖xg5! 24.♘xg5 ♕xf5, otherwise I would certainly have played it. The real question is: how come I didn't consider such a natural move?

24.h4! ♔f7 25.♕d1

Things are hopeless now, but I did not help my case with my next move.

25...♘e7 26.♘d8+

Black resigned.

I only realized during my comments how many mistakes were made during this game. But I liked Ian's idea in the opening so much that I couldn't bring myself to omit this game. And it is part of the blitz drama: get a position with complicated enough problems to solve and both players may drown in the amount of ideas to check in such a limited amount of time!

And if you are interested in seeing even earlier blunders, here's a novelty from Peter against Sasha.

SI 14.7 – B90
Peter Leko
Alexander Grischuk
Beijing blitz 2014 (15)

1.e4 c5 2.♘f3 d6 3.d4 cxd4 4.♘xd4 ♘f6 5.♘c3 a6 6.♗e3 ♘g4 7.♗c1 ♘f6 8.♗e3 ♘g4 9.♗g5 h6 10.♗h4 g5 11.♗g3 ♗g7

This is all well-known stuff. Now, instead of 12.h3, Peter's hand played:

12.f3 Which would be a great move if not for: **12...♘e3 13.♕d3 ♗xd4**

and Black won quickly afterwards.

The outcome of the women's blitz speaks for itself. Hou Yifan clinched gold with 22/30, a full 3 points ahead of Gunina and Anna Muzychuk! At first, Gunina seemed to be able to keep up with Hou, but a monstrous 8½/10 on the second day gave the World Champion a lead that could no longer be contested on the third day.

Here is a pretty decent game from the winner against one of the medallists, with some original play from both sides.

VO 7.11 – A03
Anna Muzychuk
Hou Yifan
Beijing blitz 2014 (19)

1.f4 d5 2.♘f3 c6 3.g3 ♘f6 4.♗g2 g6 5.0-0 ♗g7 6.d3 0-0 7.♕e1 d4 8.♘a3 ♘d5 9.♘c4 b5!?

10.♘a3 Better is 10.♘a5! ♕b6 11.a4.
10...♘d7 11.♗d2 ♘c5?!
11...♕b6 favours Black.
12.c3 dxc3 13.bxc3 ♕a5

14.♘b1
14.c4!? might be a decent blitz move, even though there shouldn't be enough compensation after 14...♕xa3 15.cxd5 ♗xa1 16.♕xa1 cxd5.
Best was 14.♘c2! ♗xc3 15.♗xc3 ♘xc3 16.♘e5 ♗b7 17.♘d4, with unclear play.
14...♘a4 15.♘e5 ♕b6+ 16.♔h1 ♘e3
A bit too optimistic. Hou certainly didn't want to allow e4, although I don't see a reason to be afraid of it. Still, the text-move does make sense.

17.♗xe3 ♕xe3

18.♘xc6?!
18.♗xc6 ♖b8 19.d4, and the queen is trapped, although Black should be OK after 19...♗xe5 20.♖f3 ♗xd4 21.♖xe3 ♗xe3, with decent chances.
18...♗b7 19.♘b4 ♗xg2+ 20.♔xg2 ♖ac8

21.♖f3
Black is clearly better after 21.♘d5 ♕c5 (21...♕e6! 22.e4 ♕d7 is even more accurate, but 21...♕c5 is much more natural in blitz) 22.e4 e6 23.d4 ♕d6 24.♘e3 b4.
21...♕e6 22.d4 a5 23.♘d3 b4!

After this break on the queenside things look gloomy for White.
24.♘e5 f6 25.♕d1

Unnecessary, but White's position is just too bad. Black also wins after 25.♘d3 bxc3.

25...fxe5

26.dxe5 Or 26.♕xa4 exd4 27.cxb4 ♕xe2+ and wins.

26...♘xc3 27.♘xc3 bxc3 28.♖c1 g5 29.♕a4 gxf4 30.gxf4 c2 31.♖xc2 ♕g6+

White resigned.

Which took us to the Basque event. The man of the first day was Ian Nepomniachtchi with 1½-½ wins against Etienne, Sasha and Leinier Dominguez. The real sensation was that he was not playing faster than his opponents... and it worked!

Let me show you the game that may have prevented Sasha's triptych.

SO 4.4 – C45
Ian Nepomniachtchi
Alexander Grischuk
Beijing Basque 2014 (2)

1.e4 e5 2.♘f3 ♘c6 3.d4 exd4 4.♘xd4 ♘f6 5.♘xc6 bxc6 6.e5 ♕e7 7.♕e2 ♘d5 8.c4 ♗a6 9.♘d2 g6 10.♘f3 ♘b6 11.b3 ♗g7 12.♗b2 0-0 13.0-0-0

There seems to be no end to the growth of China as a chess nation.

Ian had played this a few months ago, with good success. It looks risky at first sight, but the king has to get away from the centre and White's attack is coming on quite fast.

13...♗b7

Very natural. 13...♖ab8 14.♕d2!? ♖fd8 15.♕a5 ♗b7 16.c5 was better for White in Nepomniachtchi-Ganguly, Bilbao 2014.

14.h4

14...a5

14...h5? is met by 15.♖g1! c5 16.g4 hxg4 17.♖xg4 ♗xf3 18.♕xf3 ♗xe5. Typical for the Scotch; White is not afraid of giving up pawns for an attack or much more active pieces. After 19.♗d3 White's attack looks tremendous.

15.♕c2

I would instinctively have played 15.h5 at once.

15...a4 16.♔b1 axb3 17.axb3 c5 18.♖e1 ♖a6 19.♗d3

19...♖fa8

Bad was 19...h5? 20.♘g5 ♖fa8 21.f4! ♖a2 22.♗xg6 fxg6 23.♕xg6, and wins.

20.h5

But this is not a bad idea!

20...♖a2

The best move, according to the com-

Alexander Grischuk seems to ignore both boards, his opponent and the arbiter, in his Basque match against Shakhriyar Mamedyarov.

25.♕xe6 dxe6 26.♘g5 Black has problems defending his kingside: 26...♗c8 27.♖e3.

24.gxf3

24...♚f8?!
Stronger was 24...♕e6! 25.♖hg1 ♕xg6+ 26.♖xg6 ♚f7 27.♖g5, and despite being a piece up for the moment, Black either has to lose a lot of time getting his rooks back in play or give up an exchange. The knight on b6 is also very much under control for now, so Black faces a very tough defence.

25.♖h5
25.f4! was the most precise.

25...♕e6 26.♖f5+ ♚g8 27.♖g1 ♕xg6 28.♖xg6 ♖xb2+ 29.♚xb2 ♖f8 30.♖xf8+
30.♖fg5 ♖f7 31.f4 also looks good.

30...♚xf8 31.f4

This endgame is still very difficult to defend. The rook is better than the two minor pieces, given the number of weaknesses in Black's camp.

31...d6 32.♚c2 dxe5 33.f5 ♘d7 34.♖c6 e4 35.♖xc7 ♚e7
So far, Sasha has defended excellently in the endgame.

36.♖c6

puter, was the active 20...d5. Another fun fact about the Scotch is that you can easily drown in the amount of lines available for study, and I will show only the tip of the iceberg here. Anyway, although the text-move, 20...♖a2, looks very tempting, the rook may easily become useless in endgames, as White will instructively show.

After 20...d5 play may continue 21.hxg6 hxg6 22.♗xg6! dxc4! (22...♚f8? 23.♘h4 dxc4 24.♘f5, winning; 22...fxg6? 23.♕xg6 dxc4 24.♘g5 winning) 23.♗xf7+! ♕xf7 24.♘g5 ♕d7 25.♖d1

ANALYSIS DIAGRAM

25...♘d5 (Black loses after both 25...♕g4? 26.♖h8+ ♗xh8 27.♕h7+ and 25...♕e7? 26.♕g6! ♖a1+ 27.♚c2

cxb3+ 28.♚xb3 ♗d5+ 29.♚c2) 26.bxc4 ♖b6! 27.f4 ♘c3+! 28.♕xc3 ♕f5+ 29.♕d3 ♗c8!. This is just an unreal sequence! Black is two pawns down but suddenly has enough counterplay on the white king. And although Black's king doesn't look secure, there's just no way for White to exploit its position: 30.♘e4!? ♖ab8 31.♖d2 ♗e6 32.g4 ♕xg4 33.♚c1 ♖b4! 34.♘f6+ ♗xf6 35.exf6 ♖xc4+ 36.♗c3 ♖b1+!! 37.♚xb1 ♗f5 38.♖h8+ ♚f7 39.♖h7+ ♚f8, with a draw by repetition.

21.hxg6 hxg6 22.♗xg6 fxg6

23.♕xg6
This does look quite scary for Black!

23...♖xf3
After 23...♚f8?! 24.♖h5 ♕e6

36...♗d4?! The move was 36...♔f7!
37.♖e6 ♘e5 38.♔d2 ♘f3+ 39.♔e3
♗d4+ 40.♔xe4 ♘d2+ 41.♔d3 ♘xb3,
and Black is holding.
**37.♖e6+ ♔d8 38.♖xe4 ♗xf2
39.♔d3 ♗g3 40.♖e6**

40...♗e5

He should have tried 40...♗h4 41.♔e4
♗e7 42.♔d5 ♔e8 (this defensive set-
up was his last chance) 43.♖a6 ♔f7
44.♖a7 ♘f6+ 45.♔e5 ♘g4+.

Beijing Basque 2014				
1 Ian Nepomniachtchi	RUS	2801	7½	2747
2 Teimour Radjabov	AZE	2776	6	2770
3 Maxime Vachier-Lagrave	FRA	2728	6	2761
4 Shakhriyar Mamedyarov	AZE	2739	6	2747
5 Leinier Dominguez	CUB	2763	5½	2767
6 Alexander Grischuk	RUS	2828	5½	2760
7 Peter Leko	HUN	2773	5½	2767
8 Wang Hao	CHN	2719	5	2783
9 Levon Aronian	ARM	2813	5	2720
10 Radoslaw Wojtaszek	POL	2684	4½	2747
11 Ruslan Ponomariov	UKR	2738	4½	2742
12 Wang Yue	CHN	2765	4½	2754
13 Pentala Harikrishna	IND	2701	4	2773
14 Boris Gelfand	ISR	2719	4	2756
15 Vassily Ivanchuk	UKR	2811	3½	2740
16 Etienne Bacrot	FRA	2731	3	2751
16 players, 5 rounds				

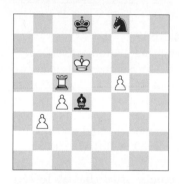

'Two gold medals and one silver would most certainly be a dream result for most players, but I am not entirely sure that the World Champion was 100 per cent happy about it!'

**41.♔e4 ♗f6 42.♔d5 ♗e7 43.♖a6
♔e8 44.♖a7 ♗h4 45.♔e6
♘f8+ 46.♔d6 ♗g3+ 47.♔c6
♗f2 48.♖b7 ♗g1 49.♔d6 ♗d4
50.♖c7 ♔d8 51.♖xc5**

White wins. The pawns will clearly be
one too many for the knight. Excellent planning by Ian.
**51...♗xc5+ 52.♔xc5 ♔c7
53.♔d5 ♘d7 54.b4 ♘b6+
55.♔d4 ♘d7 56.♔e4 ♔c6 57.c5
♔b5 58.♔d5 ♘xb4 59.c6 ♘b6+
60.♔d6 ♘b5 61.f6 ♘c4+ 62.♔e6**
Black resigned.

On the second day, Ian immediately
put an end to most of the suspense
with a 2-0 win against his closest rival
at that point, Pentala Harikrishna.
The day finished with Ian winning
another gold medal for Russia, while
I happily settled for a third podium
place. Sharing 2nd-4th place with
Shakh and Teimour Radjabov, I got
bronze, while Teimour earned silver.

While Sasha Grischuk can easily
be described as the best performer of

these Mind Games, this time I had no
reason to be disappointed with my
performance, although I felt my play
was a bit uneven at times.

For me this meant the end of
another fun event, which was also
extremely tiring. But, of course, in the
evening our trio gathered for a final
session of Pineapple Open-Face Chinese Poker, and this time we were
joined by Ian. And now, for the most
eagerly awaited result of the week!
While Sasha was wise enough not to
win here as well – although he may
not agree – I showed spectacular sta-
bility with another second place. And
newcomer Ian decided it was the day
to win it all!

In the women's Basque competition
Zhao Xue was on a roll on the first
day, scoring 5½ out of 6! Hou Yifan
gathered 5 points and was even more
merciless on the second day, when
she first beat Zhao Xue 1½-½ and
then Koneru Humpy 2-0. So a total
of 8½ from 10; not shabby at all and
good enough for first place. Two gold
medals and one silver would most
certainly be a dream result for most
players, but I am not entirely sure that
the World Champion was 100 per
cent happy about it!

Here is her best effort, with her own
comments.

**NOTES BY
Hou Yifan**

SI 19.14 – B81
**Tatiana Kosintseva
Hou Yifan**
Beijing Basque 2014 (3)

This was my third game with black
against Kosintseva in the 2014 Mind
Games. My loss in the second blitz
game with the black pieces [the first
one was a rapid game, which she
won – ed.] from a winning position
was a big disappointment for me, so
this time I was full of fighting spirit.

1.e4 c5 2.♘f3 e6 3.d4 cxd4
4.♘xd4 ♘f6 5.♘c3 d6 6.♗e3 a6
7.g4 h6 8.h3 ♘c6 9.♗g2 ♗d7
10.♕e2

A new try, which seems more precise
than the immediate 10.f4. Amazingly,
we copied the game that we played in
the 2012 Grand Prix in Kazan. Both
of us probably went for the moves we
were most familiar with. That game
continued 10.f4 ♕c7 11.♕e2 ♘a5
12.♖d1 ♘c4 13.♗c1 ♖c8. White's
expansion on the kingside didn't yield
any dividends but weakened it, which
Black later exploited [0-1, 73 – ed.].

10...♖c8 11.f4 ♕a5?!

A 'handmade' move. Unfortunately,
this is not a brilliant novelty, but just a
blunder. But it proves that an unusual
surprise, although not good, is still
effective sometimes.

The normal choice is 11...b5, of
course, hoping for some counterplay, but with the simple 12.a3 ♕c7
13.♘b3 ♗e7 14.0-0 White could
have exerted pressure on the black
position.

12.♕f2?

Walking into the trap! Starting from
here, a series of only moves will lead to

a promising position for Black. Con-
ducting two games at the same time
is more exacting for the players, and
somehow Tatiana missed the obvious
12.♘b3! ♕c7 13.♕f2 b5 14.0-0-0,
and here there's no exchange sacrifice for Black and it's White's turn to
strengthen her attack.

12...♘xd4 13.♗xd4 e5

14.♗b6?!

Tempting, but objectively speaking
unsound. No-one wants to go back to
e3, but sometimes you have to admit
your mistake if you want to survive:
14.♗e3 ♕b4 15.♗d2! (the point is
to prevent the fatal sacrifice on c3)
15...♕xb2 16.♖b1 ♕a3 17.♖b3 ♕c5
18.♕xc5 ♖xc5 19.♖xb7, and White
maintains good chances to keep an
equal position.

14...♕b4 15.0-0-0 ♖xc3 16.bxc3

16...♕a3+!

This was my idea when I moved the
queen to a5. Thanks to this check,
White's king remains in danger
all the time, which would not be
the case if you took on c3 immediately: 16...♕xc3 17.♕e3! ♕c6 (after

17...♕a1+ 18.♔d2 ♕xa2 19.♕c3,
without the 'obstacle' on c3, White's
pieces are more active and better
coordinated) 18.♖d3 ♗e7 19.♖c3
(again stressing how unwise it was to
take the c3-pawn!) 19...♕b5 20.♖c7,
with counterplay for White.

17.♔d2

The only move. After 17.♔b1 ♗e6!
only 18.♖d5 can save the position, but
that is already pointless.

17...♗e7

18.f5

Kind of wasting time, because in such
a position Black shouldn't waste a
tempo just to take the f4-pawn.
Therefore, mobilizing more pieces to
join the defence was a priority: 18.♖b1
0-0 (on 18...exf4?! 19.♗d4! opens the
game only in White's favour) 19.g5
♘h5 20.gxh6 ♖c8 when Black keeps
attacking, but things are not yet clear.

18...0-0 19.♖b1

19...♖c8?!

Too casual. Although this maintains a large advantage, Black should
have been more careful. Instead of
the text-move, 19...♗a4, in order to
prevent ♖b3 and threatening ...♖c8,
with an attack on the c3-pawn, would

Hou Yifan had good reason to rub her hands in glee, but posing in front of the Bird's Nest, the World Champion is in fact rubbing her hands together from the cold.

have been far more efficient. As far as we could see, White can do nothing against this plan. For instance, 20.♖hd1 ♖c8, and Black is winning.
20.♖b3 ♕xa2 21.♖hb1 ♕a4

22.♕e2?
This last mistake gives Black an extra tempo to finish the game quickly. 22.♕e1 was not the best, but at least it avoided some problems. Against this I had planned 22...a5! in order to control the b4-square and to prepare ...♖c4. The e4-pawn will be the pivotal point from which, under specific circumstances, Black will tear down White's defences.

Best was 22.♖b4!, when after 22...♕c6 23.♕g3 d5 24.exd5 ♘xd5 some computer lines may probably save the game, but I don't think anyone would be ready to search for such solutions at the board, especially when you have another game going at the same time!
22...♗b5

23.♖xb5
A choice inspired by the unpalatable 23.♕e1 ♗c4 24.♖b4 ♕c6, when c4 is a much more powerful square for the bishop than d7, and the ...d5 push is a mighty threat.
23...axb5 24.♖b4

Or 24.♖xb5 ♘d7 25.♗e3 ♕a1 26.♖b3 ♘c5, which is similar to the game.
24...♕a1 25.♖b3 ♘d7

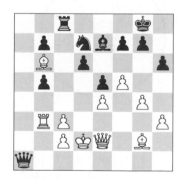

26.♕xb5
Or 26.♗e3 ♘c5 27.♖xb5 ♘a4, and Black wins.
26...♗g5+ 27.♔e2 ♘xb6 28.♕xb6 ♕c1 29.c4 ♕xc2+ 30.♔f1 ♕xc4+ 31.♔g1 ♕c1+ 32.♗f1 ♖c2 33.♖f3 ♕d2
White resigned. Opposite-coloured bishops do not necessarily lead to draws if one side is attacking! The end of this game is just a small sample of this theory. ■

The Waiting Game

Jeroen Bosch

4.h3!?

'You may be inclined to laugh at this 'beginner's' move, but Giri's 2½ out of 3 against the likes of Kramnik, Adams and Caruana was no laughing matter.'

The popularity of the Berlin Wall was once again confirmed in the London Chess Classic 2014. The six-player round robin with a 'classical' playing tempo saw five games in which Black played the queenless middlegame. And what is more, Black scored four draws and one win. The Berlin Wall is clearly the scourge of 1.e4 players these days.

In the open rapid tournament the grandmasters were more prone to experiment. Thus, runner-up Anish Giri uncorked his antidote to the Berlin Wall: 4.h3 in the Four Knights. You may be inclined to laugh at this 'beginner's' move, but his 2½ out of 3 against the likes of Kramnik, Adams and Caruana was no laughing matter. In this column we have no option but to treat 4.h3 seriously. Moreover, the philosophy behind 4.h3 is similar to that behind one of my favourite SOS lines of all times: the Gunsberg Variation, which starts with 4.a3!?.

SO 1.1 – C46
Anish Giri
Vladimir Kramnik
London rapid 2014 (6)

1.e4 e5 2.♘f3 ♘c6 3.♘c3 ♘f6 4. h3!?
Before we start investigating this waiting move properly, we should establish the philosophy behind this cyclist's approach of *sur place*. Why

would White want to spend a move on a small improvement of his position at move 4? After all, this is usually the time to develop pieces or stake your claim in the centre. Let's have a look at White's two main moves first: 4.d4 and 4.♗b5.

■ The Scotch Four Knights starts with the logical 4.d4, but after 4... exd4 5.♘xd4 ♗b4 Black obtains easy development and counterplay in view of the threat on pawn e4. The main line continues 6.♘xc6 bxc6 7.♗d3 d5 8.exd5 cxd5 9.0-0 0-0

10.♗g5, which is relevant for our discussion of 4.h3 d5, as I will demonstrate below. Actually, 10.h3, planning 11.♕f3 (from Kramnik-Aronian, Moscow 2012), is a relatively fresh idea.

■ The Spanish Four Knights is the other main attempt. The disadvantage of this developing move is most clearly shown by Rubinstein's 4.♗b5 ♘d4, attacking the bishop. Allow me to make two SOS references that are relevant to Giri's approach in London: rather than on 5.♗a4 or 5.♗c4, I once wrote an SOS column on 5.♗d3!? (SOS-11 Chapter 15). It is also interesting to play 4...♗d6 instead of 4...♘d4 (NIC 2002/6).

The idea of ...♗d6 or ♗d3 stems from the Ruy Lopez: in the so-called Arkhangelsk Variation after 3.♗b5 a6 4.♗a4 ♘f6 5.0-0 b5 6.♗b3 ♗b7 7.d3 Black now has 7...♗d6!?, which is a respectable line.

■ Another 'active' move is 4.♗c4?!, but that actually makes matters worse for White, as 4...♘xe4! is an easy equalizer for Black.

By now it should be clear that, while 4.d4 and 4.♗b5 (and, to a far lesser extent, 4.♗c4) are perfectly playable, they do give Black ideas about how to proceed and create counterplay. This is no different from Adorjan's and Suba's idea that Black is OK. Black is adjusting his plans here in accordance with the information that he is getting from White. It is therefore no surprise that some players have looked for moves that do not give Black any leverage.

■ Thus, Dutch grandmaster John van der Wiel has experimented with the

innocuous-looking 4.♗e2 (see SOS-7, Chapter 2).
■ While Russian grandmaster Igor Glek has made a career out of 4.g3.
■ My personal favourite waiting move is Gunsberg's 4.a3!?, which featured in one of the early SOS-columns in NIC 2001/8.

The philosophy behind this move is that it puts the ball in Black's court – and White can suit his reaction to Black's reply – while at the same time slightly improving White's position. A strikingly 'modern' concept from the 19th-century player (and contestant for the World title) Isidor Gunsberg. 4.a3 has prevented the 'Spanish Four Knights Reversed', of course, while 4...♗c5 is no good following 5.♘xe5. 'Slower' moves like 4...♗e7 or 4...d6 may now be met by 5.d4. Crucial, of course, is the question of how to meet 4...d5:
– 5.exd5 ♘xd5 6.♗b5 ♘xc3 7.bxc3 ♗d6 8.d4 exd4 9.cxd4 0-0 10.0-0 ♗g4 is the main line of the Scotch Four Knights with reversed colours...

... and now 11.♗e3!? has the merit that it prevents ...♘b4 (which is relevant in that line). 11.c3 would be the traditional

move, when the extra tempo (a2-a3) is certainly not to White's advantage.
– I once thought that White (after 4.a3 d5) could profitably go for the sharp lines following 5.♗b5 ♘xe4 6.♘xe5 (6.♕e2 is equal) 6...♕g5 7.♘xc6 ♕xg2 8.♖f1 a6 9.♘xd5 axb5 10.♘xc7+ ♔d7 11.♘xa8 ♕xc6, which is a theoretical position with reversed colours and without a2-a3.

I no longer think, however, that inserting the little pawn move alters the position in White's favour. In fact, Black is to be preferred. Depending upon your sense of humour, though, it is funny that after 12.♕e2 ♗c5! 13.d4 ♗xd4? (13...♗e6! favours Black) there is only one move that promises White a nearly winning edge (all others favour Black!)...

... and that move is 14.a3-a4!!: 14.a4 ♘d6 (14...bxa4 15.♖xa4 ♗h3 16.♖xd4 ♕xf1+ 17.♕xf1 ♗xf1 18.♔xf1 ♘c5 19.b4 ♘e6 20.b5+ ♔xb5 21.♖d5+ ♔c6 22.♖a5 and wins) 15.axb5+ ♔d7 16.c3 ♖e8 17.♗e3 left White a clean exchange up in Schneider-Levushkina, Nuremberg 2011. Perhaps all chess philosophy is 'more or less bunk', to paraphrase Henry Ford, and concrete moves are all that matters?

With the above the philosophy behind Giri's very own waiting move 4.h3 has been explained, while we have also prepared the ground for our discussion of that move, since many of the same themes will return.

4...♗b4

Interestingly, all of Giri's opponents opted for the 'Scotch Four Knights'. This was probably where they saw absolutely no advantage to the extra h2-h3. The young Dutchman had another surprise up his sleeve, though. We will need to investigate the alternatives as well:

■ The other 'main' answer is the Reversed Scotch Four Knights, when I think that after 4...d5 Giri's idea was 5.exd5 (5.♗b5 ♘xe4 offers no prospects) 5...♘xd5 6.♗b5 ♘xc3 7.bxc3 ♗d6 8.d4 exd4 9.cxd4 0-0 10.0-0...

... and now the traditional main line – i.e. 10...♗g4 – is obviously not on, which provides at least one argument in favour of 4.h3.

■ 4...♗c5 still allows 5.♘xe5 ♘xe5 6.d4,

although it is true that this doesn't yield all that much for White (what 'comfortably equalizes' for Black in

the opening books is often 'only equal' for White). 6...♗d6 (on 6...♗b4? 7.dxe5 ♘xe4 8.♕g4 is already winning, Emödi-Radnoti, Zalakaros 1988) 7.dxe5 (not 7.f4?, which is good after 4.a3 ♗c5 5.♘xe5 ♘xe5 6.d4 ♗d6, but is now met by 7...♗b4!) 7...♘xe5 8.♕f3!? (8.♗d3) 8...0-0 9.♗d3 ♗xc3+ 10.bxc3 d5 11.♗g5! dxe4 12.♗xe4 h6 13.♗xf6 ♕xf6 14.♕xf6 gxf6 15.0-0-0 is a tiny endgame edge, Mikhaletz-Nechaev, Khmelnitsky 2008.

■ 4...♗e7 is a bit passive, but not bad, of course. White can play 5.d4 exd4 6.♘xd4 0-0 (no good is the Scotch antidote 6...♗b4?!, as after 7.♘xc6 bxc6 8.♗d3 d5 9.exd5 cxd5 10.0-0 0-0 11.♕f3! White is a full tempo ahead of Kramnik's 2012 idea) 7.♘xc6 bxc6, and now 8.e5!,

also known via 4.a3, is the way to go. White is a touch better after 8...♘e8, and 8...♘d5 9.♘xd5 cxd5 10.♕xd5 does not give Black quite enough for the pawn: 10...♖b8 11.♗d3 ♗b7 12.♕d4 as 12...♗xg2? 13.♖g1 ♗c6 14.♖xg7+!! ♔xg7 15.♕g4+ ♔h8 16.♕f5 wins.

■ In the same category as 4...♗e7 is the solid 4...d6. The position after 5.d4 has actually occurred quite a few times, because it often arises via move orders like 1.e4 ♘c6 2.♘f3 d6 3.h3 ♘f6 4.♘c3 e5 5.d4 or 1.e4 d6 2.d4 ♘f6 3.♘c3 ♘c6 4.h3 e5 5.♘f3.
5...♗e7 (5...exd4 6.♘xd4 g6 7.♗g5!? ♗g7 8.♘d5 a6 9.c3 with a White edge, Galdunts-Miles, Bad Wörishofen 1995) 6.d5 (6.♗b5 ♗d7 7.0-0 exd4 8.♘xd4 ♘xd4 9.♕xd4 ♗xb5 10.♘xb5 yields White very little, Galkin-Michna, Warsaw 2006) 6...♘b8 7.♗e3±. A recent

grandmaster outing saw 7.g3!? 0-0 8.♗g2 c6, Ter Sahakyan-T.L.Petrosian, Yerevan ch-ARM 2014.

■ 4...g6 is the Glek Variation (reversed). White can play 5.d4 exd4 6.♘xd4 ♗g7 7.♘xc6 bxc6, with approximate equality, but note that here for the first time 5.♗c4 is a decent move, since 5...♘xe4? is a blunder due to 6.♘xe4 d5 7.♗xd5!.

■ 4...a6 continues the waiting game. Now, after 5.d4 exd4 6.♘xd4,

– 6...♗b4 7.♘xc6 bxc6 8.♗d3 d5 9.exd5 cxd5 10.0-0 0-0 11.♕f3 is Kramnik's plan once again. White is a useful tempo ahead (h3 is necessary, ...a6 isn't).

– If you are really adept at the waiting game, you will play 6...♘xe4!? here, the point being that after 7.♘xe4 (7.♘xc6 ♘xc3 8.♘xd8 ♘xd1 9.♘xf7 ♔xf7 is equal, and 9...♘xf2!? 10.♔xf2 ♔xf7 11.♗c4+ ♔g6 12.♗d3+ ♔f7 13.♗c4+ is perhaps just a draw) 7...♕e7 8.f3 d5 a theoretical position has arisen, with the added moves h2-h3 and ...a7-a6.

This favours Black, since the theoretical refutation of this line without these moves starts with 9.♗b5!.
You are a cheeky bastard if you reply

with 4...h6!?. One may wonder if this is the future of chess?

5.♗d3!?

The perfect SOS reply! Remember the SOS line 4.♗b5 ♗d6 ? Here Giri has the useful h2-h3 thrown in for good measure. This should not promise White an advantage, but he is playing with an idea in mind, which is already something. And after all, we could have been witnessing the umpteenth Berlin Wall here, right?

Another witty reply is 5.♘d5, Rubinstein's Variation with reversed colours, but unfortunately 5...♘xd5 6.exd5 e4 is an immediate equalizer.

5...0-0

Michael Adams continued with 5...d6 6.a3 ♗a5 7.b4 ♗b6 8.♘a4.

White obtains the bishop pair, but this should not upset the balance all that much in this closed position. Black is still solid, although White is pressing a little.

8...0-0 (8...♘c7 9.0-0 ♘g6 10.♘xb6 axb6 11.♖e1 ♗d7 12.♗f1 ♗c6?! 13. d4! ♗xe4 14.♗g5 ♗xf3 15.♕xf3 c6 gave White enough for the pawn in Svensk-Moberg, Sweden 2009) 9.0-0

d5 (logical, since the knight has left c3, but not entirely accurate perhaps) 10.exd5 ♕xd5 11.♖e1 (stronger was the paradoxical 11.♘c3! ♕d6 12.♖e1, and Black has some trouble holding on to his e-pawn: 12...♖e8 13.♗b2 ♗d7, and now 14.♘e4! ♘xe4 15.♗xe4 keeps White in the driver's seat) 11...♗d4! 12.♘xd4 exd4 – the position is equal.

After 13.♗f1 ♗f5?! 14.d3 a5?! 15.♗f4?! (15.g4!, followed by 16.♗g2, promises an edge) 15...axb4 16.axb4 b5? (16...♕b5!), 17.♘c5 was better for White. The game continued 17...♖xa1 18.♕xa1 h6 (18...♘xb4? 19.♖e5!) 19. g4 ♗xg4 20.hxg4 ♘xb4 21.♖e5 ♕f3 22.♗g3 ♕xg4 23.♘e4!, and White went on to win in Giri-Adams, London rapid 2014.

6.0-0 d6 7.a3

This is the logical continuation of White's set-up. Against Caruana, Giri had played 7.♖e1, and after 7...♘e7 8.♘e2 (8.a3) 8...d5?! (8...♘g6 9.c3 ♗a5 10.♗c2 c6 11.d4 would be rather similar to a famous Alekhine-Euwe game (Amsterdam 1936)) 9.♘g3 dxe4 10.♘xe4 ♘g6

11.♘xf6+ (11.♘c3!?, attacking pawn e5, is uncomfortable for Black)

11...♕xf6 12.c3 ♗d6 13.♗e4 ♗f5 14. d3!? (14.♗xb7 ♗d3! 15.♗xa8 ♖xa8 looks scary in a rapid game) 14...♗xe4 15.dxe4 ♗c5 16.♕e2 h6 17.♗e3 the game was dead equal in Giri-Caruana, London rapid 2014.

7...♗xc3

This is certainly not bad, but it leaves the bishop on d3 well-placed. However, 7...♗a5 8.b4 ♗b6 9.♘a4 is a direct transposition to the above-mentioned game Giri-Adams.

8.dxc3 ♘e7

8...d5 9.exd5 ♕xd5 (9...♘xd5 10.♖e1 gives White an edge) 10.♗g5! threatens to take on h7. White is certainly a bit better. Note that 10...e4? blunders a pawn: 11.♗xe4!.

9.a4!?

Gaining space on the queenside, and this is certainly useful in a rapid game to make your opponent think for a bit (should he allow a4-a5 or play 9...a5 himself?). The customary way of playing would be 9.♗g5 ♘g6 10.♘h4, but it does not promise much.

9...h6 10.a5 ♘g6 11.c4

Black was ready for ...d5 now, and the Dutchman continues his space grabbing on the queenside.

11...♗e6 12.♗e3 ♘d7 13.b4 ♘f4! 14.♖e1 ♕f6 15.♗f1 g5?!

This is optimistic. Black would have been fine after 15...♕g6, when 16.♘h2? fails to 16...♗xc4! 17.♗xf4 ♗xf1 18.♘h4 ♕f6 19.♗g3 ♗c4, and Black is a solid pawn up. Therefore White is forced to take on f4, and after 16.♗xf4 exf4 17.♕d2 ♕f6 is equal, as is 17.e5 ♘xe5 18.♘xe5 dxe5 19.♖xe5 ♗xh3 20.♕f3 ♗e6.

16.♔h2 ♚h8 17.g3

White is a little better now, but Kramnik's next move makes matters worse.

17...♘xh3?

Correct was 17...♘g6, or, as Anish Giri pointed out, 17...♖g8!?, a piece sacrifice which the Dutchman had no intention of accepting.

18.♗xh3 g4 19.♗g2 gxf3 20.♗xf3 ♗xc4

The point of Black's 17th move. He has won a pawn. However, pawn h6 (and his kingside in general) is weak, and White's plan is fairly simple: ♔g2 and double on the h-file.

21.♔g2 ♔g7 22.♖h1 ♖h8

23.♖h4 Good enough, I suppose, although the engines prefer 23.♖h5, when Black isn't even allowed to get rid of his h-pawn for some relief exchanges. White just continues ♕d2 and ♖a1-h1, and Black is in dire straits.

23...♘f8? The point of the previous remark is that Black could now have bailed out with 23...h5!, when 24.♕d2 ♕e6 25.♖ah1 ♘f6! ensures a bishop swap at a suitable moment:

– 26.♖xh5, and this time 26...♘xh5 27.♖xh5 ♖xh5 28.♖xh5 ♖h8 29.♖xh8 ♔xh8 30.♗xa7 gives White an extra pawn, but the opposite-coloured

bishops make it hard to gain anything substantial, especially after 30...d5.
– 26.♗g5 ♖ag8 27.♗xf6+ ♔xf6 28.♖xh5?! (too straightforward, 28.♕c3! and 28.♕e3! are harder to meet) 28...♖xh5 29.♖xh5 ♔e7 is almost equal.

24.♕d2 ♘e6

25.♕c3!

This is a strong move, preventing Kramnik's defensive idea of ...♘g5. Ironically, the same ♕d2-c3 move cost Kramnik dearly in his last-round game versus Yu Yangyi in Qatar 2014.

Yu Yangyi-Kramnik
Doha 2014
position after 20...gxf5

After 21.♕c3 a double attack on c6 and e5 cost Black a pawn. For Yu Yangyi's comments on this game see page 27. Back to the game. Following the immediate 25.♖ah1 Black has 25...♘g5!? when, after 26.♗g4! ♘xe4 27.♗xh6+ ♖xh6! 28.♕xh6+ ♕xh6 29.♖xh6 ♘g5, he is still standing.

25...♗b5 26.♖ah1 ♔f8

Now, however, 26...♘g5 runs into 27.♗xg5 hxg5 28.♖xh8 ♖xh8 29.♖xh8 ♔xh8 30.♕xc7, when it is important that after 30...♗c6? White has the win-

ning 31.a6!, while 30...♗f1+ 31.♔xf1 ♕xf3 32.♕xb7 is a winning queen ending for White.

27.♗g4! One of those moves that demonstrate the difference between a world-class player (or a powerful engine) and us mere mortals. Giri is attacking another weakness in Black's camp (pawn c7) and actively striving for opposite-coloured bishops to finish Black off in a direct attack.

After the mundane 27.♖xh6 ♖xh6 28.♖xh6 ♕g7 29.♖h4 (threatening ♗h6) 29...♔e8 30.♗g4 ♔d8! Black is a lot worse, but he has not lost yet. But in the game things are well and truly over after a few more moves.

27...♗c6 28.♗xe6! ♕xe6

29.b5!

Diverting the bishop from the diagonal and attacking c7 once more.

29...♗xb5 30.♖xh6 ♖xh6 31.♖xh6 ♕g4 32.f3!?

Playing it very safe indeed. 32.♖h8+ ♔g7 33.♖xa8, and Black has nothing, as 33...♕xe4+ is met by 34.f3.

32...♕g7 Or 32...♗f1+ 33.♔f2!.

33.♕xc7 a6 34.♕xd6+ ♔g8 35.♖h5 Black resigned. He cannot avoid losing his queen. ∎

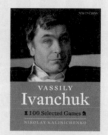
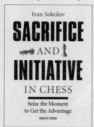

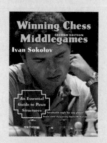
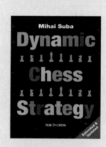

A Fairy-Tale amidst Fechin's masterworks

Two years ago he won the Moscow Open, and some people may remember that in the 2011 World Cup he reached the quarter-finals. Still, for many he must have been the great unknown in the line-up of the Russian Super-Final. Six 2700+ GMs were expected to vie for the title, but the new Russian champion's name is Igor Lysyj (2686). 'They all wanted to beat me, went in for a fight and gave me chances. And I simply exploited them,' was Lysyj's explanation of the fairy-tale that unfolded in the Khazine National Art Gallery in Kazan. **Vladimir Barsky** reports.

W When two and a half years ago Andrey Filatov suggested staging the match for the World Championship in the Tretyakov Gallery in Moscow, this seemed like the amusing whim of a rich man. But then in 2013 the Alekhine Memorial was held in The Louvre in Paris and the Russian Museum in St. Petersburg, and it transpired that the 'chess in museums' theme was very attractive. Not only for the spectators, but also for the sponsors and the players. At the end of 2013 the Russian Championship Super-Final was held in one of the museums in Nizhny Novgorod, and this year,

Igor Lysyj ponders his next move in front of a majestic painting by Nicolai Fechin. The 27-year-old GM from Yekaterinburg was the surprise winner of the Russian Super-Final.

chess themes, and during games they sketched the players. The chess tables were laid out directly in the exhibition halls. Fechin's paintings – vivid and full of colour – created a special atmosphere. One of the artist's best-known canvases is called 'Slaughter-house' – it very realistically depicts the slaughtering of cattle by the method of throat-cutting. The male participants in the Super-Final remained fairly indifferent to this work of art: 16 decisive games out of 45 is a normal percentage for high-class tournaments.

The tournament in Kazan comprised the five winners of the qualifying Premier League, the three prize-winners from the preceding Super-Final, and two players with the highest ratings. True, Vladimir Kramnik was missing. This year, because of the change in leadership of the Russian Chess Federation, for a long time the exact dates of the Super-Final remained uncertain, and the ex-World Champion had signed up for the Qatar Masters Open. Alexander Grischuk did not come for personal reasons. All our remaining stars arrived: the seven-times Russian champion Peter Svidler, Sergey Karjakin, Ian Nepomniachtchi, Dmitry Jakovenko and Alexander Morozevich. However, to everyone's surprise the winner was a 'high society' debutant, the 27-year-old grandmaster from Yekaterinburg, Igor Lysyj, who reached the Super-Final from the qualifying event (where, incidentally, he also took first place).

Igor is a native of Yekaterinburg, a large industrial city in the Urals. At the age of six he was taught chess by his grandfather. Igor was lucky with his first trainer – he was a pupil of Ludmila Saunina, a grandmaster who was several times champion of Russia. Although it is customarily thought that the main thing for a first trainer is to impart a love for chess, it is very useful at the outset to set a correct direction for development, since re-learning is always more difficult

when Andrey Filatov became head of the Russian Chess Federation, he had no choice but to continue what had been begun. As a result the best players in the country found themselves in Kazan, or more precisely – within the precincts of the Khazine National Art Gallery, which is inside the local Kremlin.

The Khazine houses the largest collection in the world of paintings by the famous Russian-American artist Nicolai Fechin (1881-1955), a native of Kazan. A well-known collector of paintings, drawings and sculptures by Russian and Soviet masters, Filatov also has several of his works. Specially for the Super-Final a monograph about the life and work of Fechin was published in English and French. In addition, students of the Kazan Art School, named after Fechin, prepared an exhibition of works with than learning. Igor remembers all his trainers with gratitude: national master Alexander Khmelnitsky and grandmasters Leonid Totsky and Maxim Sorokin (he died tragically in 2007 in a car accident on the road from Elista to the airport in Volgograd). For the last 12 years he has been helped by international master Nikolai Ogloblin, who was also Lysyj's second in Kazan.

I have known Igor for about 10 years, since the time when he was competing in junior events. Already then he was an excellent blitz player and was famed for his serious research in the openings, but even so he was overshadowed by his contemporaries. He was usually outshone by Evgeny Tomashevsky, Nikita Vitiugov, Boris Grachev and Artyom Ilyin. Later Igor entered the Ural Federal University and studied there for many years, competing in numerous student championships. Why, one might ask, fight again and again for the title of student champion of Russia or even the world – was this not a futile waste of time? But Igor continued working hard (although he liked to talk ironically about himself, saying 'I am already a veteran'), and successes came his way: he qualified for the 2011 World Cup and reached the last eight, where he lost to Leinier Dominguez only in the Armageddon game. Early in 2012 Igor won the Moscow Open, when for the first time he gave a big interview to the author of these lines. Not wishing to show off, Igor said quite sincerely: 'Chess is my life. Writing articles, playing in tournaments, seconding and training work – all this is associated with chess. Most of all I like analysing: for the moment my analytical work is better than my practical results. But, of course, I very much like winning!'

Indeed, Igor Lysyj is an excellent theoretician, and the books *The Open Games for Black* and *The Berlin Defence*, written jointly with grandmaster Roman Ovechkin, have been widely praised not only by amateurs,

but also by professionals. In Kazan the winner of the Premier League was initially underestimated, at times his opponents rather impudently played for a win against him both with White, and with Black, and Igor made excellent use of the chances that came his way.

QP 5.5 - A46
Nikita Vitiugov
Igor Lysyj
Kazan 2014 (1)

1.d4 ♘f6 2.♘f3 e6 3.♗f4 c5 4.e3 ♘c6 5.♘c3!?

Nikita has known his opponent since childhood, so that he knows better how to fight against Igor. But even so the choice of opening is extravagant, to put it mildly. It has always seemed to me that Vitiugov has a leaning towards classical play.

5...cxd4 6.exd4 ♗b4

The battle revolves around the d5-square: Black does not want to allow the enemy pawn to go there, or to place his own there.

7.♗d3 0-0 8.0-0 ♗e7 9.♘e4 ♕b6!

From the very first moves there is extremely concrete play; for

the moment White has two pawns hanging.

10.♘xf6+ ♗xf6

11.c3?! White overestimates his chances. 11.♗d6 ♗e7 12.♗xe7 ♘xe7 13.♕c1 d6 was better, with approximate equality.

11...♕xb2! 12.♗d6 ♗e7 13.♗xh7+ ♔xh7 14.♕d3+ g6 15.♖fb1 ♕xa1 16.♖xa1 ♗xd6 17.c4 b6 18.♖e1 ♗a6

For the queen Black has gained more than sufficient compensation – a rook and two bishops.

Subsequently Lysyj perhaps did not act in the optimal way, but nevertheless he gradually neutralized the opponent's initiative and converted his material advantage.

The second-round Lysyj-Svidler game ended in a draw without particular adventures, after which the Yekaterinburg grandmaster played uncertainly against Dmitry Jakovenko and lost in 25 moves. His next opponent was Alexander Morozevich, who at that moment was in sole first place with 2½ points out of three. And he wanted to build on his success...

QI 1.3 – E11
Igor Lysyj
Alexander Morozevich
Kazan 2014 (4)

1.d4 ♘f6 2.c4 e6 3.♘f3 ♗b4+ 4.♗d2 ♗e7 A rare continuation. Alexander evidently chose the Bogo-Indian Defence aiming for a complicated battle. The classical 4...♕e7 and the super-solid 4...♗xd2+ 5.♕xd2 d5 are more popular.
5.♘c3 0-0 6.a3
This is most probably a rather mediocre choice. It can be explained by my defeat in the previous round and a desire to play safely. In a normal fighting mood it would be difficult to avoid the obvious 6.e4 d5 7.e5 ♘e4 8.cxd5 exd5 9.♗d3 ♘xd2 10.♕xd2, with some advantage. In my view, Black's two bishops do not fully neutralize White's advantage in space.

6...b6!? After the game I thought that this move was the initial cause of Black's problems. But in analysis I have been unable to disclose any substantial drawbacks to it.
In the event of 6...d5 play could have transposed into theoretical lines of the Queen's Gambit after 7.♗f4.
7.e4 d5 8.cxd5
The move order is important. 8.e5?! is much weaker in view of 8...♘e4 9.cxd5 ♘xc3 10.♗xc3 ♕xd5, when after the exchange of bishops on a6 Black will have an easy game.
8...exd5

9.e5?! Strangely enough, after this natural move White should have lost his opening initiative. He should have played 9.exd5! ♘xd5 10.♗d3 ♗b7 11.0-0 ♘d7 12.♖e1 ♘xc3 13.♗xc3 ♗d5 14.♘e5, with the better game for White.
9...♘e4 10.♗d3

10...♗b7?
A serious mistake. On b7 the bishop runs up against its own pawn and is transformed into a passive piece.
After 10...♘xc3 I have been unable to find a way for White to fight for an advantage.
11.0-0 c5 12.♖e1

12...♘xc3?
This mistake could have put Black in a critical position. It was essential to play 12...♘xd2 13.♕xd2 c4 14.♗c2 ♘a6 15.e6 fxe6 16.♖xe6 ♘c7 17.♖e3, with an unpleasant, but quite playable position.

13.♗xc3? An error in reply. I was planning the variation with the e5-e6 breakthrough which occurred in the game, and I decided that after ...c5-c4 my bishop would be able to come into play via b4. But I did not take account of my opponent's rejoinder on the 17th move.
A player with a normal chess culture was obliged, without thinking, to play 13.bxc3 and conduct a mating attack against the black king:

ANALYSIS DIAGRAM

A) 13...♘c6? 14.dxc5 bxc5 (14...♗xc5 15.♗xh7+!) 15.♕b1, and White is winning;
B) 13...c4 14.♗c2 ♘c6 15.♕b1 g6 16.♗h6 ♖e8 17.e6, and White is better.
13...c4 14.♗f5?! As has already been said, White was suffering from a delusion about the strength of the e5-e6 breakthrough. Otherwise he could have played 14.♗c2 ♗c8 15.♘d2 b5 16.♘f1 ♘c6 17.♘e3 with the idea of advancing the f-pawn.

14...♗c8 15.e6

15...fxe6

In the event of 15...♘c6?! White would have had to find the only way to gain an advantage:

ANALYSIS DIAGRAM

16.♕c2! g6 17.exf7+ ♔xf7! (17...♖xf7 18.♗xg6, winning) 18.♕a4! ♗xf5 19.♕xc6 with the idea of exploiting the weakening of the dark squares after the exchange of the dark-squared bishops via b4. I doubt whether I would have been able to solve this problem, since in my calculations I was inclining towards 16.♕a4.

It is interesting to note that the other capture on e6, 15...♗xe6?, loses to 16.♖xe6 fxe6 17.♗xe6+ ♔h8 18.♘e5.

16.♗xe6+ ♗xe6 17.♖xe6

17...♘a6! This is the whole point. I looked at other continuations, which did indeed lead to a big advantage for White, but I overlooked the development of the knight on the edge of the board.

White is better after 17...♗f6 18.♕a4 ♕d7 19.♕xd7 ♘xd7 20.♖d6 or 17...♕d7 18.♖xe7 ♕xe7 19.♗b4 ♕e8 20.♗xf8 ♔xf8 21.♘e5. And he would be winning after 17...♘d7 18.♕e2 ♗f6 19.♗b4 ♕e8 20.♖e1.

18.♘e5

Despite the mistake in the calculation of the variation, White's pieces are excellently centralized and Black has to play accurately to maintain the balance.

18...♗f6?!

Stronger was 18...♗d6 19.♕d2 ♘c7 20.♖xd6 ♕xd6 21.♗b4 ♕f6 22.♗xf8 ♖xf8 23.g3, when White has merely a slight initiative thanks to his knight on e5 and the somewhat weakened position of the black king.

19.♕h5?

The natural desire to take control of the e8-square and prepare the activation of the queen's rook proves incorrect.

There were two ways available to White for gaining an advantage:
– 19.♕e2 ♘c7 20.♖c6 ♘b5, with the idea of 21.♖xc4 ♗xe5 22.dxe5 dxc4 23.♕xc4+ ♖f7 24.♕xb5, or
– 19.f4 ♘c7 20.♖c6 ♘b5, with the idea of 21.a4! ♘xc3 22.bxc3 ♕e8 23.♕f3 ♖d8 24.♖c7 ♗xe5 25.dxe5 ♖f7 26.♖xf7 ♕xf7 27.♖d1.

19...♘c7 20.♖c6

20...♗xe5? This mistake decides the outcome of the game.

Black would have emerged unscathed after the straightforward 20...♘b5! 21.a4 ♘xc3 22.bxc3 ♗xe5 23.dxe5 ♕e8 24.♕xe8 ♖axe8 25.♖e1 ♖c8 26.♖d6 ♖fd8 27.♖d1 ♖xd6 28.exd6 ♔f7 29.♖xd5 ♔e6 30.♖d4 ♔d7, and thanks to his counterplay on the queenside Black maintains the balance.

21.dxe5 ♘b5

White wins after 21...♕d7 22.♖d6 ♕f7 23.♕xf7+ ♖xf7 24.♖d1.

22.♖d1

22...♖c8? The last important moment in the game. Black's mistake involves a simple oversight.

22...♕d7 was not possible on account of 23.♖xc4, but he could have tried to save himself in the difficult rook endgame after 22...♘xc3! 23.bxc3 ♕e8 24.♕xe8 ♖axe8 25.♖xd5 ♖f5 26.♖xc4 ♖fxe5 27.♖xe5 ♖xe5. After the game Alexander said that he had seen this possibility, but thought that the resulting endgame was lost.

23.♖xc8 ♕xc8 24.♖xd5 ♕c6

25.♕d1

As Alexander admitted, it was this queen move that he had not taken account of in his calculations. I cannot say that my opponent's words greatly surprised me. I noticed long ago that backwards moves by the strongest piece are often overlooked in the calculation of variations.

25...♘c7

25...♘xc3 26.bxc3 also loses.

26.♖d7 ♘e6 27.♗b4

White forces the black rook to take up a passive position.

27...♖e8 28.♖d6 ♕b5 29.♗c3

29...♘f4

Morozevich, as usual, complicates matters and seeks chances right to the very end. I am pleased that, with time somewhat limited, I was able to work out the consequences of the winning variation which occurred in the game.

Igor Lysyj: 'I cannot say that my opponent's words greatly surprised me. I noticed long ago that backwards moves by the strongest piece are often overlooked in the calculation of variations.'

30.♕g4 ♘d5 31.♖d7 g6 32.♕h3 h5 33.e6 ♖e7 In the event of 33...♘xc3 34.♕xc3 ♕xd7 35.exd7, the white queen is controlling the e1-square. **34.♖d8+ ♖e8 35.♕f3** Black resigned.

■ ■ ■

'They all wanted to beat me, went in for a fight and gave me chances. And I simply exploited them', was how Igor Lysyj modestly explained his success. In the fifth round he had Black against the rating favourite. Karjakin was on –1 and he very much wanted to break the unfavourable course of the tournament.

Sergey Karjakin - Igor Lysyj
position after 22.♗a1

White has gone in for a grand battle, but Lysyj shows that he has a subtle understanding of 'hedgehog' nuances. **22...e5!** 'Black cannot mark time for the entire game and move here and there, because in the end White will nevertheless squeeze his position. He has to break out!' (Lysyj). It should be added that at this moment Karjakin was already short of time, so that Lysyj's sharpening of the play was very opportune.

23.♘c2 b5 24.cxb5 axb5 25.♘b4 ♘e6

'I think that objectively Black is not worse. And in addition, the position is not at all easy for White to play' (Lysyj).

26.♕f2

In the event of 26.♗f1 Black can play 26...♘d4, setting a little trap: if 27.♘e2? there follows 27...♗h6! 28.♕xh6 ♘xf3+, and White's position collapses.

26...♗f8 27.♘cd5 ♘xd5 28. exd5 ♘f4 29.♗f1 ♖c8 30.♗b2 ♕c7 31.♗c1 ♕a5 32.♗d2 ♕a3 33.♗xf4! exf4 34.♖xe8 ♖xe8 35.♘c6

35...b4

Apparently 35...♖e3!? was more accurate, for example: 36.♗xb5 ♕c5 37.♗a4 ♗g7 38.♔g2 (38.b4 ♕b6) 38...♗c3 with a strong initiative for Black.

36.♖d4? In time-trouble Sergey takes an unsuccessful decision. After the simple 36.♗c4 ♗g7 37.♖e1 White is not worse, and he can even play to seize the initiative: 36.♕d2! ♗g7 37.♘xb4 ♖c8 38.♗c4 ♖xc4 39.bxc4 ♗c3 40.♘c2 ♕c5+ 41.♕f2 ♕xc4 42. a3. The black bishops are very strong, but even so White is the exchange up. **36...♗g7!**

37.♖c4 37.♖xb4 is not possible because of 37...♗xc6, while in the event of 37.♖xf4!? White was probably afraid of 37...♗xc6 38.dxc6 d5!, but then 39.g5 ♕c1 40.♖xb4 ♕xg5+ 41.♔h2, and there is still all to play for. **37...♗c3!**

38.♕c2?

The decisive mistake. 38.♔g2! was essential, with the idea of 38...♗xc6 39.dxc6 d5 40.♖c5, when there is no deadly check from d4.

38...♗xc6! 39.dxc6

In the event of 39.♖xc6 ♕a5 40.♗c4 ♕d8! 41.♔h2 ♖e1 checkmate on the dark squares is not far off.

39...d5

40.♖xc3

40.♖xf4 ♕a7+ 41.♕f2 ♕c7 or 41.♔g2 ♕e3 also fails to save White. **40...bxc3 41.♕xc3 ♕a7+ 42.♔g2 ♕xa2+ 43.♔g1 ♕a7+ 44.♔g2 d4 45.♕c2 ♕a5 46.♗c4 ♕c3 47.♕f2 d3 48.c7 d2**

And White resigned.

Emboldened, in the next round Igor also defeated Denis Khismatullin, after which he was not simply leading the race, but was now a whole point ahead of his closest pursuers. But then he came unstuck against the resourceful Vadim Zviagintsev.

Vadim Zviagintsev - Igor Lysyj
position after 28.♗xb7

Black cannot regain the pawn immediately by 28...♗xb3 on account of

Kazan 2014				1	2	3	4	5	6	7	8	9	10		cat. XIX
															TPR
1 Igor Lysyj	IGM	RUS	2686	*	0	½	½	1	1	1	0	½	1	5½	2795
2 Dmitry Jakovenko	IGM	RUS	2745	1	*	½	½	½	½	½	½	½	½	5	2751
3 Peter Svidler	IGM	RUS	2743	½	½	*	½	½	½	0	1	½	½	4½	2708
4 Ian Nepomniachtchi	IGM	RUS	2714	½	½	½	*	½	0	½	½	½	1	4½	2712
5 Denis Khismatullin	IGM	RUS	2679	0	½	½	½	*	1	1	0	½	½	4½	2716
6 Nikita Vitiugov	IGM	RUS	2738	0	½	½	1	0	*	½	1	½	½	4½	2709
7 Alexander Morozevich	IGM	RUS	2724	0	½	1	½	0	½	*	½	1	½	4½	2711
8 Vadim Zviagintsev	IGM	RUS	2655	1	½	0	½	1	0	½	*	½	0	4	2675
9 Boris Grachev	IGM	RUS	2669	½	½	½	½	½	½	0	½	*	½	4	2674
10 Sergey Karjakin	IGM	RUS	2770	0	½	½	0	½	½	½	1	½	*	4	2662

29.♗c6, and the same move follows after 28...♖d7. There begins a complicated 'dance' of bishops and rooks, with mutual attacks and discoveries. **28...♗a3 29.♖a1 ♗e7 30.♗b6 ♖b8 31.♔g2 ♗xb3 32.♗e3**

32...♗d6?
Here any human player's head would be spinning, but the computer demonstrates a subtle way to draw: 32...♗b2 33.♖ab1 ♗a4!! 34.♖e2 ♗e5 35.♖xb8+ ♗xb8 36.♖a2 ♗d7 37.♖a8 ♖e8.

33.♖a6!
A brilliant intermediate move, the aim of which is to dislodge the bishop from the a3-f8 diagonal.

33...♗c7
Black's downfall is caused by the numerous pins and the absence of an escape square for his king. For example: 33...♖d8 34.♖b1 ♗e6 35.♖xd6 or 33...♗b4 34.♖b1 ♗c2 35.♖xb4. After 33...♖e6 34.♖xd6! ♖xd6 35.♗f4 ♖dd8 36.♗xb8 ♖xb8 37.♖b1 Black is unable to disentangle himself: 37...♖b5 38.♗c6 ♖b4 39.♗d5. There is the very pretty variation 33...♗e5 34.♖b1! ♖d7! (threatening an exchange on d1) 35.♗a7! ♖b4

The top three finishers that gained the right to appear in the next Super-Final without qualifying: Denis Khismatullin (3), Dmitry Jakovenko (2) and champion Igor Lysyj.

ETERI KUBLASHVILI

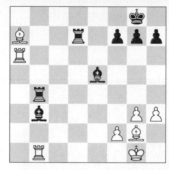

ANALYSIS DIAGRAM

36.♗b6!, cutting off the rook from the b8-square. Black has a tempo to safeguard his king, but after 36...h6 37.♖a8+ ♔h7 38.♗a5! ♖b5 39.♗c6 he loses a rook.
34.♖b1 ♗e5
34...♖ee8 is met by the already familiar manoeuvre 35.♗a7! ♖b4 36.♖a3.
35.♖a3 ♗c4 36.♖xb8+ ♗xb8 37.♖a8 It is a pin that decides the game, not vertical but horizontal. Black resigned.

Nevertheless, the battle in the tournament was so tight, that by making two draws in rounds 8 and 9 Igor Lysyj took sole first place.

Half a point behind the winner was Dmitry Jakovenko, the only player to go through the whole tournament undefeated, his only win com-

ing in fact against the future champion. This is the fourth 'silver' in championships of the country for the grandmaster from Nizhnevartovsk, but for the moment first place continues to tantalize with its gold allure. On the other hand, there is something to aim for!

As many as five players finished on fifty per cent. Thanks to the best tiebreak, third place, giving the right to appear in the next Super-Final without having to qualify, was gained by the grandmaster from Neftekamsk, Denis Khismatullin. For him, as for Lysyj, for the moment this is the biggest success in his career. Ian Nepomniachtchi, Peter Svidler, Alexander Morozevich and Nikita Vitiugov finished outside the prize-winners. In the second round Nepomniachtchi defeated Karjakin, after beginning the game with Bird's Opening (1.f4!?), but he was unable to build on his success. He very much wanted to catch the leader, and in the last round against Vitiugov he overstepped the mark. Svidler, like his compatriot and colleague, returned to 50% only in the last round. Morozevich performed unevenly: at the start he won two games in succession, then he lost two in succession, and in the end the pluses and minuses in his play evened themselves out. ■

Of Openings and Bishop Snatchers

I t's not easy making people happy with opening books. If I compare the situation with 10 years ago (when I last reviewed books for New In Chess), then the standard of opening books has improved beyond recognition. In the past couple of years I have reviewed books that I would have killed for as a professional or as a young player. To give just a small sample, Quality Chess' books on the Tarrasch, the French and most recently on a 1.e4 repertoire are phenomenal works. And yet... a trawl of the forums often throws up some surprising comments. I've often been shocked to read (sometimes quite bitterly-phrased) complaints that a particular opening book is too detailed, too difficult, overly complex.

If I've had a tough week at work, then I'll often scream something rude at the screen when I read comments like that. Something like 'But chess *is* complicated and difficult! Every sub-sub-variation of an opening has been tried out in at least 50 or 60 high-level games. The author has clearly spent months working on the book and has already cut down the material to a fraction. Why should you expect then to be able to master this just by a quick flick through the pages?'

Once I calm down though, I do understand the point that is being made. As an amateur, your entire preparation takes place on the morning before the game. If you're lucky,

you'll have a pretty good idea against whom you might play, which might allow you to prepare an opening a bit more specifically. If you're playing in the Dutch league, then you might as well not bother! It's just like cramming for an exam. What you're really looking for is something that tells you quickly what to play, and makes the judgment for you of what you need to know and what you can work out at the board. Books in the Quality Chess

> 'If you like to set yourself a challenge then the Modern is for you. (It's such an awesome opening.)'

range are probably out of the range of amateur players from that point of view, but then I don't think that the 'last-minute-learn-it-quickly-for-the-game' market is the one Quality Chess is aiming at. I got thinking about this after dipping into *The Modern Tiger* by Tiger Hillarp Persson (Quality Chess). When I started playing chess again, one of the openings I took up

was the Modern. I reached that decision via a relentless process of logic: 'Who didn't know anything about opening theory? Dave Norwood. What did he play? The Modern. Right, let's do that then!' When you come across a book like Tiger's with 500 pages of deep analysis and superb explanation, you suddenly realise how vulnerable you were when you played the opening in that state of blissful ignorance!

In his witty and thought-provoking preface, Tiger alludes to how the information explosion has altered the way he views and plays the Modern.

'When I played Tiger's Modern 10 years ago, I was a different chess player from what I am today, and more so than anything in relation to the opening that this book is about. Back then I thought, "Everyone should play the Modern – it's such an awesome opening!" whereas my attitude today is more along the lines of: "If you like to set yourself a challenge then the Modern is for you. (It's such an awesome opening.)"

'I used to know almost no "theory" on the Modern before I wrote a book about it, but I still managed to achieve

The Modern Tiger
Tiger Hillarp Persson
Quality Chess, 2014

good results. However, since then the …a6 Modern has received more attention, and it has become more difficult to use it as a weapon of surprise. Today it's more important to be well-prepared and know a number of concrete lines.

'Before the era of super-strong engines I was happy to play a complex and unclear position more than once, whereas now I prefer not to repeat these lines too often, because I do not want to get involved in lines that my opponent might have analysed for hours with an engine.'

It is an absolutely super book. One of my favourite pastimes in the past month has been just to open the book and look at the diagrams and see how many pieces Black is missing (OK then, has sacrificed!) and in how many games Black has castled (…♔f8-g8-h7 doesn't count!). You have to be quite a special sort of player to play this opening, but you'll probably have a lot of fun if you get it right. The last word has to be Tiger's:

'This is not the tale of the "ugly duckling", where in the end we come to realise that the duckling is in fact a swan. No this duck is a duck, but I like this duck. It's a unique duck in its own right, and it may even turn into a hippopotamus!' Four stars!

★★★★

Watch out with *The Secret Life of Bad Bishops* by Esben Lund (Quality Chess). I've had a number of non-chess players wanting to borrow the book hoping for steamy tales of sinful prelates! It's a – by modern stand-

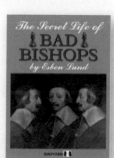

The Secret Life of Bad Bishops
Esben Lund
Quality Chess, 2014

ards – shortish book (192 pages) that essentially covers one theme, or rather one new definition. The concept of the 'bad bishop' has always been confusing and even divisive. Try telling a French expert that his light-squared bishop is bad…

… and he'll hit back with an example of a glorious light-squared bishop winning the game:

(a game Agzamov-Kosikov, Orenburg 1972, annotated in Dvoretsky's *Training for the Tournament Player*) Or take Black's dark-squared in the King's Indian…

No King's Indian specialist will ever look to swap off the hemmed-in bishop on g7 when it might do this…

(from Timman-Kasparov, Linares 1992)

Lund resolves this problem by coining a new term: the 'Double-Edged Bishop' (DEB), which he defines as 'a bishop that cannot yet be declared good or bad, but rather holds the potential of becoming good as well as the risk of becoming bad'.

When I read this, I was very happy! It's one of those wonderful moments when something you have understood intuitively is explained clearly and concisely and a little part of chess suddenly makes a bit more conscious sense. The only danger in such a book is that once you hear the concept, you just think 'Ah yes! Of course, that's right! Phew, glad that's cleared up!' and then put the book aside. I'm afraid that's what I did the first time, but I'm glad I came back to the book again because Lund provides an awful lot of interesting content related to this theme. In particular I liked Lund's point about the importance of being aware of the DEB's in your position and in your opponent's position and of the effect that exchanges can have on the 'goodness' or 'badness' of the DEB. Thoroughly recommended and

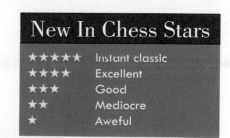

New In Chess Stars	
★★★★★	Instant classic
★★★★	Excellent
★★★	Good
★★	Mediocre
★	Aweful

makes a very nice change from trying to memorise opening variations. I'll give that Angelina Jolie, Brad Pitt, Michelle Pfeiffer and Christian Bale.

★★★★

Evgeny Sveshnikov's *Sveshnikov vs the Anti-Sicilians* is another fine book, continuing the series of books that Sveshnikov is writing for New In Chess on the Sicilian. Having spent my professional career in continuous frustration at not getting my Najdorf *again*, it's nice to see a book dedicated to making White's life unpleasant in these systems! The great thing about Sveshnikov's books is that he still actively plays the openings he recommends and he is still as fanatical as ever about the correct way to play openings. The introductory chapter, in which he takes Mark Dvoretsky to task for admiring his pupil Zviagintsev's invention of 2.♘a3, and scolds Bezgodov and Soloviov a little for devoting so much attention to 2.a3, shows the passion that drives him in his choices of openings.

I've never quite understood the success of these anti-Sicilians to be honest. I mean, take a look at this system:
1.e4 c5 2.♘c3 ♘c6 3.♗b5 ♘d4 4.♗c4 e6 5.♘ge2 ♘f6 6.0-0 a6 7.d3 b5 8.♗b3 ♘xb3 9.axb3 ♗b7

White has wasted 3 moves in the opening with his light-squared bishop only to get it exchanged. Even with the current state of my openings, I still turn my nose up at *that* position. Why isn't White just a tad worse here? But Aronian, Tiviakov, Movsesian, Vallejo have all played it so I

guess there must be something in it… No, sorry, still can't believe it!

Sveshnikov's choice of openings against the anti-Sicilians is always very principled, trying to challenge White's setup straightaway. For example, there is a very interesting section on 1.e4 c5 2.g3 d5…

… which I always considered a little too risky for Black in my professional days, but Sveshnikov makes a very good case for it. His analysis of this variation:
1.e4 c5 2.♘c3 ♘c6 3.♘f3 e5

is probably the best part of the book. There are so many interesting King's Gambit type possibilities! For example, this one was new to me:
1.e4 c5 2.♘c3 ♘c6 3.♘f3 e5 4.♗c4 ♗e7 5.d3 ♘f6 6.♘g5 0-0 7.f4 d5 8.♘xd5 ♘xd5 9.♗xd5 exf4

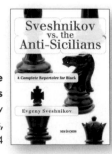

Sveshnikov vs the Anti-Sicilians
Evgeny Sveshnikov
New In Chess,
2014

10.♘f3 ♗h4+ 11.♔f1

I had always thought this line to be quite dull and boring for Black (I played it once as a professional and then gave it up after a rather depressing loss against Tony Kosten) but this seems more like it!

One word of caution. Although you can play these lines whichever

> 'The great thing about Sveshnikov's books is that he still actively plays the openings he recommends.'

system of the Sicilian you want to play against the Main Lines, Sveshnikov assumes that you really want to play his system: 1.e4 c5 2.♘f3 ♘c6 3.d4 cxd4 4.♘xd4 e5. That's the reason he recommends lines such as 1.e4 c5 2.♘c3 ♘c6 3.♘ge2 e5. If you were planning to play the Richter-Rauzer, for example, you might well be happy just to play 3…♘f6 in that position. So depending on your desired Main Line Sicilian system, you might well want to mix and match. Warmly recommended though! Four stars!

★★★★

Finally two books which deal with patterns in chess: *Improve Your Chess Pattern Recognition* by Arthur van de Oudeweetering (New In Chess) and *Chess Analytics* by Efstratios Grivas (Russell Enterprises). Both are pretty good books! They both present 40 chess themes and illustrate them with many lightly-annotated games. You have to give both the authors a lot of credit. Though the themes are very familiar, they are illustrated with lots of games that were unfamiliar to me. It's been a joy working through these examples and coming across yet another unfamiliar gem. In terms of 'sitting-on-the-couch-and – enjoying-flicking-through-it – ability', then Van de Oudeweetering's book just edges it. Grivas' book is a little denser and would need a little more serious work to get through, while Van de Oudeweetering's book can be read just for fun! That might have something to do with the expressive titles he chooses for his chapters: 'A Not So Innocent Bystander', 'The Beastly Bishop' or (my favourite) 'The Bishop Snatcher'. In fact, I was continually exclaiming 'Oh I've had a game like that!' while reading it, so that's probably a good indication that it's a stimulating read. Just to round off, I'll just show you a couple of the associations the book brought up with me:

Theme 38: A Double-Edged Exchange: ♗x♘c6

This theme concerns White giving up the light-squared bishop protecting his king for a knight on the queenside. For me, this theme is forever associated with this game:

Polugaevsky-Sadler
France 1993

Improve your Chess Pattern Recognition
Arthur van de Oudeweetering
New in Chess, 2014

I was pretty happy with the way I had played up till now and was also enjoying my position. 20.fxg5 ♘e5 is strong for Black so I felt that the white king was going to get uncomfortable very quickly. Polugaevsky's solution was very nice: he was very proud of it himself after the game, and rightly so!

20.♗xc6

20...bxc6 21.♕xc6 g4 22.hxg4 fxg4 23.♔g3

Many things have changed in the position and I didn't adjust well even though I had enough time. White is a little better here anyway. ♗xc6 has given White's pieces some nice soft entry squares in the black position: the queen is nicely settled on c6 while d5 is now also White's to occupy with the knight. And even more worryingly –

and this I only realised once it was too late – Black's king is the one in danger, not White's!

23...♕f5 24.e4 ♕f6 25.♗e3 h5 26.♖h1 ♕h6 27.♘d5 ♔h8

Not the world's most perspicacious choice I fear. The position was very difficult already however and I was looking for some tricks with ...♗e5 or ...♖e5, for which I needed to be able to take the knight on d5 without allowing a check.

28.♖h2 ♗xd5 29.cxd5 ♗f6 30.♖ah1 ♖e5 31.♕c1 h4+ 32.♖xh4 ♗xh4+ 33.♖xh4 ♖h5 34.♗d4+

1–0. Wonderful coordination from White's pieces and a very good game from Polu!

Theme 25: The Bishop Snatcher

This theme is about the exchange sacrifice ♖xe6, snatching off a bishop on e6. This brings up another trauma!

Ivo Timmermans
Matthew Sadler
Netherlands 2011

1.e4 g6 2.d4 ♗g7 3.♘c3 c6 4.♘f3 d5 5.h3 ♘h6 6.♗f4 dxe4 7.♘xe4

♘f5 8.c3 0-0 9.♗d3 ♘d7 10.0-0 ♘f6 11.♖e1 ♘xe4 12.♗xe4 ♘d6 13.♗c2

The sort of moment in the game where you put on a sour face and wish you'd handled the opening a little differently! Black is a little passive. Now comes one of those practical moments when you think. 'Would he? Or wouldn't he?' I decided my opponent wouldn't...

13...♗e6

14.♖xe6

Curses! He did!
14...fxe6 15.♘g5 ♕b6 16.♘xe6

♕xb2 17.♗b3 ♔h8 18.♖c1

This was more unpleasant, and less murky, than I'd realised. White has a really good position! A lot more moves were played, many of them with only a tenuous connection to correctness. Eventually we reached this position:
33.g4

After unwisely accepting a second very creative exchange sacrifice, I am completely lost. However, for the first time in the game, I spotted something!
33...♖f7 34.♕xg6 ♖ef8 35.♕h6+ ♔g8 36.♕g6+ ♔h8 37.♕h6+ ♔g8 38.♕g6+ ½-½.
White decided to take the draw by repetition. It's one of those times when

you're not sure whether you should be happy or upset. The point is that while 37.g5 and 37.f4 win for White, 37.♗c2 (threatening 38.♕h6+ ♔g8 39.♗h7+ mating) certainly does not...!

ANALYSIS DIAGRAM AFTER 37.♗C2

I don't want to have to show all my losses and lucky escapes so I think I'll stop there with the themes! Four stars for Van de Oudeweetering and we'll saw Brad Pitt in half to give Grivas three and a half stars.

★★★★
★★★⯪

Chess Analytics
Efstratios Grivas
Russell Enterprises,
2012

COLOPHON

PUBLISHER: Allard Hoogland
EDITORS-IN-CHIEF:
Dirk Jan ten Geuzendam, Jan Timman
CONTRIBUTING EDITOR: Anish Giri
EDITORS: Peter Boel, René Olthof
ART-DIRECTION: Jan Scholtus
PRODUCTION: Joop de Groot
TRANSLATORS:
Sarah Hurst, Ken Neat, Piet Verhagen
SALES AND ADVERTISING: Remmelt Otten

© No part of this magazine may be reproduced, stored in a retrieval system or transmitted in any form or by any means, recording or otherwise, without the prior permission of the publisher.

NEW IN CHESS
P.O. BOX 1093
1810 KB ALKMAAR
THE NETHERLANDS

PHONE: 00-31-(0)72-51 27 137
FAX: 00-31-(0)72-51 58 234
E-MAIL:
SUBSCRIPTIONS: nic@newinchess.com
EDITORS: editors@newinchess.com
SALES AND ADVERTISING:
otten@newinchess.com

BANK DETAILS:
IBAN: NL41ABNA 0589126024
BIC: ABNANL2A in favour of Interchess BV, Alkmaar, The Netherlands

WWW.NEWINCHESS.COM

1. Gormally-Granda Zuniga
Isle of Man 2014

16.♘h6! This funny leap wins on the spot as both 16...gxh6 and 16...♕g6 will be met by 17.♗h5. Black resigned.

4. Rambaldi-Delchev
Bad Wiessee 2014

20.♘xg7! ♔xg7 21.♖xf6! ♔xf6 22.♕f2+ ♔g7 22...♔e7 23.♗xc5+ loses the queen – an important detail. **23.♗h6+!** The queen is coming to f6, with devastating effect. Black resigned.

7. Hayrapetyan-Khairullin
St. Petersburg 2014

31.c7 ♖c8 32.♕xc8! ♖xc8 33.♘xc8 ♕c5 34.♘d6! ♕xc7 35.♖f8+ Black resigned. 35...♔g7 36.♘e8+.

2. Sos Andreu-Petrov
Malta 2014

Black's last move 26...♖a8-a7 kept the a-pawn but led to a more serious loss. **27.e7! ♔f7 28.♗d5+ ♔xe7 29.♖f1** Cursing his c-pawn, Black resigned.

5. Barrero-Granda Zuniga
Spain 2014

35...♖xd5! 36.♕xd5 ♕f6+ 37.♔g1 ♕xf1+! 38.♔xf1 ♘xe3+ 39.♔e1 ♘xd5 40.e4 ♘c7 0-1.

8. Acs-Brunner
Mitropa Cup 2014

54.♕e3! Black resigned. His pieces are overloaded and heavy material losses are unavoidable.

3. Areshchenko-Vidit
Lake Sevan 2014

47...c3! 48.♕xc3 ♕f1+ 49.♕c1 ♗c2+! The right square for the bishop! Both White's major pieces are pinned while 50.♔xc2 loses to 50...♖c8+. Therefore, he resigned.

6. Kotronias-Banikas
Isthmia 2014

25...♖xh3! 26.gxh3 ♕xe4+! 27.♖xe4 ♘f6 White resigned as the weakness of the long diagonal will cost him the rook and the queen.

9. Meins-Kunin
Germany 2014

Twice as instructive as the previous one. No need to try and create an attack along White's back rank. **30...♖xc6!** White resigned in view of 31.bxc6 ♕b8+.

Alejandro Ramirez

CURRENT ELO: 2595

DATE OF BIRTH: June 21, 1988

PLACE OF BIRTH: San Jose, Costa Rica

PLACE OF RESIDENCE: Dallas, Texas, USA

What is your favourite colour?
Some shade of blue.

What kind of food makes you happy?
Mexican aguachile, Peruvian ceviche, Sichuanese Hot-Pot. I like spicy and full of flavour. Please no bland Euro-food.

And what drink?
What drink or how many?

What is your favourite book?
A Short History of Nearly Everything by Bill Bryson.

And your all-time favourite movie?
Amélie, with Audrey Tautou.

What is your favourite TV series?
Game of Thrones. All time maybe *Death Note*.

What music do you like to listen to?
Some kind of alternative rock, either in English or Spanish.

Do you have a favourite artist?
Hiyao Miyazaki.

What was your best result ever?
My 2nd place at the US Championship in 2013.

What was the best game you have ever played?
Eh, maybe my win against Eljanov in Aeroflot eons ago.

Who is your favourite chess player?
As a chess player, Kasparov always struck me as what every chess player should strive to be. However, to relax, have a drink and go over a chess game with, the best player by far is Morozevich.

Is there a chess book that has had a profound influence on you?
I read *Think Like a Grandmaster* maybe 30 times when I was nine years old. I'm not sure if that was a good thing or not. Benko's *Endgame Laboratory* compilation book is the reason I knew endgames as a kid.

What was the most exciting chess game you have ever seen?
Morozevich-MVL from Biel 2009 is the most WTF game I've ever seen.

What is the best chess country in the world?
Probably still Russia, though I hope some other country takes up this baton soon.

What are chess players particularly good at (except for chess)?
Thinking they are right when they are not, and making a compelling case for it.

Do chess players have typical shortcomings?
They generally know nothing outside of chess. This, of course, has strong exceptions, as there are players with immense cultural and academic knowledge, but they seem to be the exception that confirms the rule more than anything else.

What is it that you appreciate most in a person?
Honesty. Also, and relevant since I'm from Latin America, punctuality has never hurt anyone.

What is it that you dislike in a person?
Ambivalence.

Who or what would you like to be if you weren't yourself?
I like being myself actually. How about myself and some extra money in the bank account and a house in Waikiki Beach? ☺

Which three people would you like to invite for dinner?
John Oliver, Rex Sinquefield and Elizabeth Warren would be a nice hotpot.

Is there something you'd love to learn?
Chinese, dancing Salsa, how to cook more ethnic food, how to differentiate one wine from another… come on, there's so much in this world…

What is your greatest fear?
Hurting people I care about due to stupidity.

What would you save from your house if it were on fire?
My cats!

How do you relax?
If I ever feel too relaxed, I start up *Hearthstone* or *Starcraft* and get my stress levels up. I do enjoy the occasional read or binge-watching anime.

Is a knowledge of chess useful in everyday life?
Up to a point. Tournaments teach harsh life lessons fast in a brutal but civilized way, while solving puzzles seems to keep a brain active. Knowing the latest theory on the Najdorf? Not so much.

What is the best thing that was ever said about chess?
'You can check out any time you like, but you can never leave!' Wait, maybe that was about something else…

JUST CHECKING